7 Financial Cheat Codes

Live Smart, Pay Less Tax, Retire Early, and Have the Financial Freedom You Dream About

MICHAEL A. HUGGINS

Michael A. Huggins

DEDICATION

Dedicated to Socialist government policies, Wall Street, the banking institutions, and the American education system—shame on you!

Michael A. Huggins

Table of Contents

REGISTER THIS BOOK

Register your book and get free updates and free videos.

Visit www.MichaelAHuggins.com or text your name and email address to 801-899-6001.

When your book is registered you will get updates to this book plus access to videos showing you how to grow your business with strategies from this book. You will also get an invitation to an interactive online webinar to meet the author and his team.

FOREWORD

Life is complex.

There are basic patterns, algorithms, and formulas to describe and bring order to the complexity of life. We find these patterns all around us.

Consider these examples:

- Of the estimated 753,971 words in the English language, a mere twenty-six letters comprise each and every possible word.
- Of the infinity of numbers created, all of them can be generated from ten digits—zero through nine.
- Countless piano songs exist from Sarah Hale's *Mary Had a Little Lamb* to Beethoven's *5ᵗʰ symphony*, and all can be played on just eighty-eight keys.
- An estimated 2,109,386 songs have been published since 1940. Countless more unpublished songs exist because of the advent of social media sites like YouTube. Amazingly, every song

could be played on a single instrument like the electric guitar consisting of a simple six strings.

- Even our DNA, the genetic code for life itself is only comprised of six nucleic acid bases. Just look at the variety and abundance of different people on this earth!

Ernő Rubik invented one of the most popular three-dimensional puzzles in history. His Rubik's Cube has been in television shows and in movies. It is undoubtedly the most well known toy with over 350 million units sold. Well over a billion people have touched a Rubik's cube at one time or another in their life.

This simple three inch cube has over forty-three quintillion combinations (43,252,003,274,489,856,000 to be precise). However, the cube can be solved by using only seven algorithms (seven specific steps). In fact, in 2008, nineteen-year-old Erik Akkersdijk in the Netherlands, set the world record for solving it in 7.08 seconds. Yes, just over seven seconds. Children as young as four have been able to solve it by understanding the seven simple algorithms. When you learn these seven algorithms, which are really seven simple steps, you can solve the cube within two minutes. And no, one of the steps is not pulling it apart and putting it back together.

Just like the Rubik's cube, our finances are a myriad of facets, preferences, opinions, and habits. However, there is an algorithm to explain how we can get more out of our money.

In fact, these 7 Cheat Codes have been outlined by real estate investor Michael Huggins in this book.

In his book, you will learn to:

1. Set the Arena
2. Define Your Objective
3. Power Up – by starting your own business
4. Multiply Your Income
5. Annihilate Your Opponent
6. Replenish Your Health
7. Protect Your Base
8. And continue through Life Time Learning.

Just like the twenty-six letter alphabet makes up thousands of words, the 7 Cheat Codes have the ability to increase your happiness and make you more money.

~ Woody Woodward
Award Winning Film Maker, Author, Success Strategist

Michael A. Huggins

ACKNOWLEDGEMENTS

I would like to thank Woody Woodward and Garrett Gunderson for the push to get this book written. This work would not have been possible without the help of my editor Kate Frank, thank you for your expertise and knowledge. Thank you also to my publishers Jenn Foster and Melanie Johnson from Elite Online Publishing. Thank you Pall Maul and Gianfranco Fernandez for your time and attention and for being awesome. I want to thank all of you who have been supportive of my goals and dreams. I am grateful to all of those with whom I have had the pleasure to work with during this and other related projects. I also want to thank Bob Snyder and the members of Team Elevate. I would like to thank my Mom, whose love and guidance is with me in whatever I pursue. Most importantly, I wish to thank my loving and supportive wife, Vanessa, who provides me with daily motivation and inspiration.

INTRODUCTION
SET THE ARENA

My life, contrary to popular opinion, began on planet Earth.

I share this with you because if I leave some parts out you might think me alien. You might think it all just happened—dumb luck statistics. You might think me "born this way". You might come up with a bunch of excuses about why it worked for me and why it won't work for you. I figure if I give you this detail, if I give you this information, some of it might spark something in you to give you permission to change. After all, you all started on earth, too.

"Our only limitations are the ones we set up in our own mind."

– Napoleon Hill

I come from a loving family, but with a scarcity mindset

regarding money. The same one monopolizes you and your family, I'm sure. And without me thinking about it, a certain belief kind of impressed itself upon me, imposed, really; our family believed us poor because the people in comparison the maybe-not-earth-born people are rich.

The belief was the justification for being poor. Not that we ever discussed money much, but I picked up from my mom's language when she had conversations with other adults: "We are poor because others are not." That was the belief.

It was frustrating.

We Are Poor

What's this thing called allowance other kids get growing up? No such thing as allowance in my house. We hardly ever eat at restaurants; we don't do school lunch, to expensive an event.

My mom figured out a way to pack us a little something. Every once in a while, there'd be a treat in there, a Rice Krispie or Fruit Roll-up. I didn't recognize the blessing at the time; the silver lining in this: I never developed an addiction to candy, soda, or chips!

With this limited mindset controlling my then current paradigm, I looked for free stuff. Hand outs worked just fine, and so I would often ask "You done with that?"

Experiencing a cash flow challenge, home offered little to eat. I remember weeks and months where I took a bit of food from ten different friends like a collection. I'd get a bite of pizza, hot dog and a taco—*variety*. I tried to get a bit of everyone's food so I wouldn't be hungry or have to eat too much of the little at home for the rest of the day. That's how broke my family was.

Imagine being the oldest of four (and maybe you are!) and not knowing your dad. Never meeting him. Not knowing what he looks like. Not knowing his name. Not knowing him at all. That's me; there's no image of my father in my head. No attachment to good or bad, and there are pros and cons that come with that. I think it's great that I never had to fill any voids from having him come in and out. *It's just mom. Mom is here. Mom does this.* And that's where the focus went. It is what it is.

When I was in the fourth or fifth grade, my mom went back to school. She had a mental breakdown because she couldn't juggle parenting, going to school and doing the full-time job and all the mess included with it all. We ended up in a foster home for about two weeks while our grandparents figured out all the legal paperwork.

We lived with one set of grandparents for six months in Utah and the other set of grandparents in California. The experience exposed me to a different world. It was interesting. For one thing, having a male role model in the home created a hard shift for me.

My grandpa differed from my mom callously. I remember one day when my brother and I were just goofing around jumping on the bed, my grandpa came into the room and said, "Cut that out or I'm going to whip your ass." Based on my experience with my mom, I thought, *Ha, I've heard this before. Whatever.*

Five minutes go by before we start jumping on the bed again —Grandpa came into the room, took off his belt and whipped our asses ... both of ours. Oh my God did it hurt! It really set the tone —when grandpa says don't do something he means it.

After a year of living with grandparents, my mom got her act together and we moved back with her. My mom worked two jobs and went to school. She did a full 40 and would also work another shift at a different hospital. She was "on call" which meant she had to be at the hospital within 15 minutes if the hospital called. Sometimes my mom would just say, "Gotta go, party over. Get your stuff and let's go." It was a little frustrating.

Xbox Live Adventures

When I was 14, after years of begging, Mom got us an Xbox game console. I became obsessed with a game called MechAssault. Since my mom worked the night shift, she didn't know how much I played.

One day I heard the voice of this girl in the game, she was playing live along with me and others. I'll tell you a secret, for just a voice I immediately thought she was hot. She played the game well, too. I soon learned she lived in Salt Lake City—a commonality. We sent private messages through the gaming system and she gave me her phone number. We texted back and forth even though I had no idea how to talk to girls.

My neighbor, who also played the game felt I should meet her. One night he got a hold of my phone and started messaging the girl. The party was over and we were headed home about 2am when my friend pulled over, reached into the back seat to get my phone, "Hey,," he started, "you see the car back there? That's the girl. She wants to meet you."

I looked like a bum and worst I smelled like one. My neighbor pushed me out of the car and I started my strut over to her car and got in. I saw this beautiful young lady with long, black hair, a beautiful smile and a cute pink shirt and the nicest, sweetest voice I was on sensory overload.

Although I was not representing myself accurately, she gave me a ride home and said, "Let's hang out tomorrow after you get some rest." Vanessa and I became really good friends and played that video game all the time. Our moms decided we both needed to get jobs. So we walked into Wendy's fast food and got jobs.

Since we were working, we decided to get our own place. It was low income housing downtown, kind of a slummy place. We had no idea what it'd be like to pay bills. We had no idea what it was like to pay *a* bill! One day the lights went out. At first we thought it a power outage. We looked at each other, "Well, we're smart. We can figure this out." We talked our neighbor into letting us run an extension cord from their apartment. With that power strip we got by for a couple of days.

All the money we made went to the rent and we couldn't keep living that way. I started working for my grandpa in construction. Two jobs, an apartment and no car. I was a mess, but I was living and having fun.

After graduating from high school, I considered my options and leaned into automotive. Mostly I wanted to help my mom. When something broke on the car, I saw sometimes up to 80 percent of the bill was labor. I figured I could help my mom and grandpa if I learned how to fix the car.

I met a recruiter from a technical college who told me I could make $80,000 a year as a certified mechanic. Since I never wanted a desk job, the idea made sense. I moved to California to attend the tech school. Vanessa stayed back in Utah and we talked several times a day.

Since I still did not know how to manage my money and pay bills, even with the roommate arranged by the tech school, we were evicted. We ended up homeless, living in my roommate's 2-door Honda SE, parked in the lot of the school. We were never late for class and I went back to asking several friends for a bite of their food.

I got pretty skinny, but I didn't want my family to know. I just figured, *if I get through school with good grades, I can get a good job and everything will turn around.* The school in California stopped offering my degree and I had to transfer to Arizona. This time I wanted Vanessa to come with me. I traded an old laptop I found for a 22 year old van and within 24 hours, we were off to Arizona. The roof leaked, but it got us to Phoenix.

Vanessa gets a full-time job and I get two part-time jobs. I worked in a restaurant and a movie theater. One of my managers called me a "free loader." I quickly justified myself as an "opportunist" instead. Justification is a mental disease.

Most of my life I had been in school with merit and future hanging on whether I got good grades. But, I believed that with good grades I could slack off in other areas of my life. Such a flawed philosophy.

The Law of Compensation does not let you get away with such thinking for long. It keeps track of everything. Our apartment was burglarized and we lost all our electronics. It sucked, but we ignored the signals.

All around me were signals it was time to make a change. I was being dishonest with my employer by taking food. I was being dishonest at the movie theater by letting fifteen friends sneak in every single weekend.

In this life, there is no such thing as "something for nothing." Everything has a price.

Move Back to Utah

After I graduated, we moved back to Utah. We moved into Vanessa's mom's basement and I assembled friends to rent the whole house. She moved out and we moved in. (This turned out to be a huge tax benefit for her and turned a tax bill into a tax refund.)

After bouncing around from shop to shop, I finally landed at Jiffy Lube and the student loan payments kicked in at $760 a month. At first it was fun, then the winter hit with snow and rain making it pretty miserable. To top it all off, I didn't have a car. After a long day of working on cars and busting my ass, I would have a 30-minute bike ride to get home. 30-minute bike ride!

It sucked. I was working with negative people, convicts and kids. They transferred me all around the valley. All I knew was I needed two jobs because working more time meant more money. It wasn't enough so I started selling plasma twice a week after work. I made $280 a month but I was still eating bologna and garbage bread. When you're trying to work 17+ hours a day without proper nutrition it starts to take a toll on you.

Big Paradigm Shift

After saving up the plasma money for months and months, I took Vanessa to the Florida Keys. January vacation meant a break from the cold. It was amazing. On the trip there, I got my hands on a health and fitness magazine and read it from cover to cover. I started learning about pesticides; modified food starch; corn starch; guar gum; xanthan gum; and all the fillers used to make the food look bigger and tastier without it having any food value at all.

I started learning about the quality of meat, the branched chain amino acids and everything else. Since one of my goals was to live to 100 and have vitality the whole time, learning about nutrient deficiencies leading to illness was a revelation to me.

I became obsessed with health and fitness. I earned an amazing body. I had an amazing six pack. My biceps were huge. My shoulders were great. Working on cars wasn't hard because I had all these extra muscles. I cleaned up my food and stopped drinking alcohol. I wasn't interested in parties anymore—all because of the one trip to the Keys and reading the magazine. But man, was I a jerk still. I had the crummy attitude that "It's okay for me to steal." I would steal fitness magazines from the grocery store.

One time, instead of stealing the fitness magazine, I took a success magazine. I thumbed through it searching for ways to make more money and thought this magazine could help. I was in the parking lot, in a borrowed car, looking at the magazine. In the back, I found a CD and put it in thinking I would get to listen to music. It starts with music then some voice, "Welcome to success. We're here to inspire you and change your life. Enjoy this clip from a speech by Jim Rohn."

Jim Rohn asked me to walk away from the 97 percent and not talk like they talk. He said don't do what they do. Don't use their language. Don't use their excuses. Don't use their method of drift and neglect. They won't even walk around the block for their health. They won't even eat an apple a day. They won't even take time to refine their philosophy for a better life. Walk away and join the 3 percent. Be part of the few.

As I was listening I was like, "What the heck is he saying to me?"

He goes on to say, "Develop a whole new language. I don't care if it starts with a book or a journal or it starts with a walk around the block or an apple a day. Get it started. Start a journal that when people read it they will say 'This is the study of a serious student.' They're going to be powerful."

I'm like, *Whoa*. Floored. Things are just firing off in my brain.

He continued, "Once you look back on it, you will never go back to the old ways and the old language and the old neglect." Jim Rohn's 3 minute, 50 second speech changed everything. Ev-ery-thing!

I listened to the CD at least three more times before I left the parking lot. I was already doing jump rope first thing in the morning and eating an apple a day. But I didn't know it had to do with retirement. Rohn said every discipline affects every other discipline. He's telling me if I can be healthy, I can be wealthy. So I walked away and joined the 3 percent.

I start studying Tony Robbins, Les Brown and Zig Ziglar every day and I was pretty excited about life.

In the summer of 2010, I borrowed a laptop to make a payment on my student loan and found the two years of giving them $16,000 had not reduced the amount I owed. All the payments were going to interest.

I was so mad. I was mad at myself because I felt like a fool. I was mad at Sallie Mae. I was mad at the government. I wanted to blame my mom because she told me to go to college. I was mad at the people who encouraged me to get a student loan.

I wanted to blame, but I knew better. Jim Rohn told me you're not supposed to blame. But I felt stuck in this loop. I am not in the mood to sleep. I see an infomercial about how to make money with real estate. I decide right then and there, no matter what anyone thinks or says I am going to be a real estate investor. I took what little money I had in the bank and ordered a book for $29.99.

As I begin reading it, the book said I have to make sacrifices for things to change for me. I must be willing to give up good for great. *Sacrifice, huh*. I was like, *Okay*.

He made a really good argument in the book saying poor people watch TV. Poor people play video games. Poor people waste their time with things like that. I realized the TV was costing me. The 97 percent were watching TV and I needed to walk away from them. So, on my next day off, I drove out to the west desert and blew the TV to pieces with a shotgun.

Real Estate Beginning

A couple of weeks after I got the book someone calls. They tell me I should buy their program because it would help me make even more money. They promised me a coach and an 800 number for support. They said they would train me about how to find and make deals in real estate.

As I read through the success stories I was confident if these people could do it, I could do it too. I worked out a payment plan where I was going to pay $500 a month for the next 12 months in order to get this $6,000 training program. I started working Sundays to pay for it. I was maxed out with working 7 days and 70 hours a week.

The guys at Jiffy Lube asked, "Who are you? What are you talking about? You can't do real estate." The book had prepared me for the comments so I was not discouraged. When I got to my second job at Sears, I started talking about my plans and got the interest of the service writer named Nick. It turns out we both went to the same stupid school and got the same stupid student loan and then the same stupid job. Nick told me he had been wanting to figure out this real estate thing too.

Nick and I tried roadside signs, spending what little money and time we had with no results. We would walk through open houses with no clear idea of what we were doing. We looked in the newspapers to find opportunities. There, in the back and at the bottom of the page in the real estate section—a message: "Real Estate Investor Seeks Trainee."

Real Estate Training

I immediately called. Like the magazine read on the plane, this call changed my paradigm and my life again. I was nervous and kept telling myself "You got this." The lady who answered the phone began asking a few questions about why I called on the ad and what I did for a living. I was like, "Well, I called because I believe I'm going to be the next best candidate for you. You said you were seeking trainees and I'm the best. Right now I am a robot at an auto shop and I want to change my life. I'm sick and tired of that and don't want to do it anymore."

Jody was a very high energy lady and I loved it. I told her a little more, sharing I wanted to be a millionaire and had been reading books about real estate. She said she had an opportunity with a room for a couple more people for a private investor meeting. She wanted to know if I would show up and I made the decision to show up for everything.

I went to a secondhand store and found a shirt and tie. For the first time, I learned how to tie a tie. I borrowed a car and showed up at the first meeting. I was antsy, but I walked proudly into the meeting room. People greeted me with "Hey, we're meeting over here. Come on in."

I was just excited they let me in. I watched the presenter talk about short sales, fix and flips and pre-foreclosures. I was sold. Everyone was dressed professionally. They were polite. I thought "I am not around this many polite people ever in my life. This is incredible!"

They said it would take $20k to join and announced the next meeting. This one guy named Christian Sadler comes up and says something like, "Hey, if there's anything I can do to help you out, here's my card. Let me know." His card said, "I'm connected with every professional in the real estate industry." I was impressed.

After the meeting Jody asks a little more about me and politely asks me to enroll. I knew I had no freaking way of paying for this. With all the hours I worked on two jobs, I was barely making 30 grand a year. So I'm sitting and thinking, thinking and sitting. Finally I told her I didn't know how I would be able to do it. She offered to give me a couple of ideas. She shows me the 401K strategy, which we will cover in this book. I am blown away by the concept. She tells me about a retirement plan workshop coming up and I agreed to come and bring others.

When I got my tax refund in February 2011, I enrolled in the basic training with Renatus. I loved it! It was very different than other training course I paid so much money for. As an incentive, I made up my mind to stop shaving until I closed on a profitable deal.

Major Life Shift

I woke up early in the morning and stayed up late at night to watch training videos. I was so freaking tired all the time, so I took 10-minute naps during my 15-minute breaks. I had made a bed out of those little red rags we used at Jiffy Lube in the little storage attic above the office. I started eating my lunch up there too, so I could listen to audio books during my lunch break.

As I was about to climb down the ladder for work, I heard the words of Brian Tracy. It was another revolutionary paradigm shift where things would never be the same. He says, "Always pay full price for full value. Do not be proud of a discount at the expense of someone else." It was the day I stopped stealing. I committed to not stealing for the rest of my life. I don't steal.

The one idea changed it for me. By paying full price for full value, it keeps everything in balance with the rest of your life. It was why I didn't have any money before. The Law of Compensation was balancing things out in other areas of my life. I didn't deserve a car. I didn't deserve a steady paycheck. I didn't deserve a savings account. All this stuff because I was still okay with stealing.

I cleaned it up that day.

New Beginning

On April 1, 2011 we bought our first house, our primary residence. We cleaned up errors in judgment and continued learning. I plugged into the community of real estate investors and began looking for a profitable deal. After several months we bought a short sale with no out-of-pocket money. A few months later we sold it and made $21k profit. Before we closed on the first, we found another and made $8k ... basically replacing my job income. I gave my two-weeks notice and entered a whole new world. Vanessa was excited to kiss me after I shaved my lop-sided Amish beard.

Now we've been able to travel the world, pay off our mortgage, acquire more rentals, fortify a family trust, get my dream car, spend time when and how we want, smash obstacles and limits, multiplying our income 14 times. We are going to get to how, it's not as hard as it seems. It starts with learning from people that know more than you—really learning.

I had committed to the philosophy taught by Jim Rohn to work harder on myself than I did on my job and made a fortune. I am now coaching hundreds of thousands of people to do the same thing. I don't care about your background. I don't care about your age, your gender, your religion, your sexual orientation, your skin color, your hair length, your successes or your failures. If you are hungry like I was hungry, I will pour into you. I will sow into you so you can start to change and revolutionize your life. I'm here to make a fortune and inspire you guys and gals to take action to live your life, not by default—but by design.

Here's a déjà vu that should click more this time than the first —I share this with you because if I leave some parts out you might think me alien. You might think it all just happened—dumb luck statistics. You might think me "born this way". You might come up with a bunch of excuses about why it worked for me and why it won't work for you. I figure if I give you this detail, if I give you this information, some of it might spark something in you to give you permission to change. After all, you all started on earth, too.

I'm sharing this with you because you may be lost. You may have a spouse who has some incredible potential but they are just beat up by life. Maybe you could share my story with them and your relationship can start to blossom into greatness, start to bring more value into each of your lives. What would that be like? I'm sharing this with you because, at the end of the day, If I can do it—you definitely can.

Take back your existence or die like a punk.

CHEAT CODE #1
DEFINE YOUR OBJECTIVE

"Once you make a decision, the universe conspires to make it happen."
- Ralph Waldo Emerson

Mind of Steel

Let's go over a successful mindset.

To give us a good premise about creating wealth and avoiding financial traps, we have got to have a successful mindset. We must have a mind of steel.

The first part about having a mind of steel is you must be relentlessly positive. There's so much garbage going on in the world. People are complaining about this and that. Taxes, retirement accounts and interest rates, politics and presidents, and all sorts of stuff. People can complain, complain, complain and what's funny is people think the complaining is doing something about the problem.

Let's not fall into that trap. It's what mediocre people do. It's what average poor people do. It's what people of a limited mindset think. When we're trying to separate ourselves between a wealthy and poor mindset, we must understand a few differentiating factors. Wealthy mindset never complains, never justifies and never blames. They don't complain because they own it. They are responsible. When you take on responsibility, it's going to give you more power. Taking responsibility will give you more energy and more vision to be able to see clearly over your mistakes. Too many people try to avoid making a mistake. That's not how life works. You must make mistakes! You must fail forward. Think about every major achievement on this planet. People had to make mistakes along the way.

Implementing this practice will make a huge difference. You don't have to make a lot of money. You don't have to have an amazing business and assets and all this stuff to start implementing this rule. You implement the rule now. Then the business, the relationships, the money, the influence, the power and all that comes after. Never justify, blame or complain. That's a wealthy mindset. That's a mind of steel.

"He who is not everyday conquering some fear has not learned the secret of life"
- Ralph Waldo Emerson

Fear

Building my business thus far has been amazing. I've been able to travel all across the country and internationally. I have been able to speak to new people about taking control of their finances and avoiding these traps. People will tell you, "Do this, do this and do this." They will forget to say, "Don't do this, don't do this and don't do that." They also forget to break down all of the this-es.

There is a balance to both of these and becoming financially free is ultimately everyone's own responsibility. I wrote this book so you can find some value, take advantage of this and create financial freedom by avoiding some of these traps millions, even billions of people have fallen into.

I think the most common question I get is, "Is there any way to do this without making mistakes or looking stupid?" The answer is no.

Every major achievement, every major accomplishment any human has done was accomplished through making mistakes and looking stupid along the way. One of my mistakes was thinking before I take any steps, I want to have every single step in mind. I want to understand it perfectly and then I'll take some action. How silly is that? It never works!

A lot of people are saying to me, "What's step eight, nine, ten, eleven and twelve?" And all I have to say is, "None of it matters until you take step one. When you take step one, step two becomes obvious and clear. When you take step two, step three becomes obvious and clear.

The vast majority of it is just moving through your fear. We were only born into this world with two fears: We're born with a fear of falling and a fear of loud noises. That's what we get as humans.

Every other fear besides these two, are fears you have taken on and adopted throughout your life. You've either put the fear there yourself or you've allowed someone else to set the fear up for you.

• Are you afraid of talking to people?

• Are you afraid of making money?

• Are you afraid of losing money?

• Are you afraid of looking stupid?

• Are you afraid of being alone?

• Are you afraid of spiders?

All those fears are something you put there or accepted from someone else. What we have to do is override the system because what ultimately happens when we experience a fear feeling is our mind sends a signal to run. It's called the fight or flight signal. The immediate reaction is, "We're about to die!"

"If you think you can, you can. And if you think you can't, you're right."
-Henry Ford

Intellectually and logically we understand making a phone call to a homeowner to ask if they are ready to sell their house at the price we are offering is not going to kill us. We don't need to fight or flee in the situation. If we aren't developed to understand this thing called fear, it's going to control us.

What I want you to do is separate the two in your mind. The easiest way to do it is to imagine two buckets in your mind. One bucket is labeled, "This will kill me." The other bucket is labeled,

"This will grow me." Now, imagine you're riding a motorcycle in a canyon at night while it's raining. You are experiencing fear. Obviously we will put this fear in the "This can kill me" bucket. It's a legitimate fear.

What about taking on a class? What about buying a piece of property? What about asking someone out on a date? What about creating a new business? What about switching jobs? What about self-directing your retirement account?

So many people experience fear with those things, but it is the kind of fear that will grow you. We need to manually separate the two in our minds. When we experience fear and the physical reaction to fear, you've got to ask yourself: "Will this kill me or will this grow me?"

If it will kill you, don't do it. But if it'll grow you, then do it. Do it now. Do it fast. Do it hard. Do it big and just go for it. That's ultimately what's going to eliminate the fear. Ralph Waldo Emerson said, "Do the thing and you will have the power." The number one thing I find, going across the country, is people allow fear to stop them. They accept fear instead of getting their dream. They decide to live with the fear.

There are two ways to look at fear. You've probably heard this one:

False **E**vidence **A**ppearing **R**eal

Here's what I suggest:

Face **E**verything **A**nd **R**ise

Do you want to have False Evidence Appearing Real or do you want to Face Everything And Rise? Which is more empowering? After learning about this way to look at fear and moving through it, I'm addicted to the powerful feeling. That's something I would encourage you to do. If you need anyone's permission, you have my permission to move through your fear.

"You must do the very thing you think you cannot do."
- Eleanor Roosevelt

Desire

People often ask me how I got started in real estate investing and sales. My answer is always the same. It started with desire. Even though the business and the money came much later, my desire to travel the world and have a secure living situation was what pushed me to become better and grow into the person I am today. It all starts with the desire. So you think to yourself:

•What do you desire in life?

•What do you desire with your time?

•What do you desire with your money?

•What do you desire with your family, your relationships and your health?

Now, some people in your world are going to make you feel like pursuing money is evil, or that money is the root of all evil. They might act as if you're out to get a whole bunch of money and intend to step on people or scam people. They think you're going to ruin things in order to get money. It's not the case at all.

The only way to get money is to add massive value to people and to the marketplace. If you're making a lot of money, wonderful – you're valuable. If you're not making a lot of money, you're not very valuable to the marketplace.

Figuring out how to become more valuable to the marketplace starts by moving through all the things you want to complete in your life. Include everything you've ever thought about. Know if you have a desire for something unique to you – it is yours. You need to pursue it. You've never been given a desire you didn't already deserve. If you've convinced yourself otherwise, well that's what I'm here for. If you felt it and it's your desire, you deserve it and you need to go for it.

As soon as you have a desire and start moving forward, guess what? The next thing is going to be an obstacle. Henry Ford said, "Obstacles are those ugly things you see when you take your eyes off of your goal."

Just know obstacles are going to come up no matter what. Every. Single. Time.

Think about this. Say you decide to be a professional boxer but don't want to get punched in the face. That's not going to work. Or say you want to have a really fit body, but you don't like sweating. Maybe you want to make a whole lot of money, but you don't want to talk to anyone. These things are all contradictory.

What's interesting is, we create many of the obstacles we face in life. We make up excuses about time. We make up excuses about skill-sets and abilities. We start saying things like, "Well, I've never

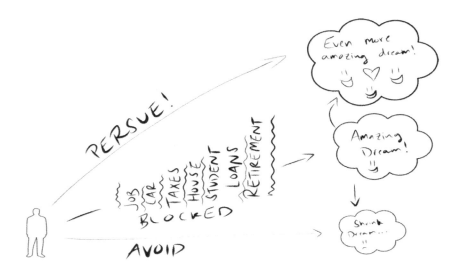

done it in the past, so I can't do it in the future. I've never done it before, so I don't think I can ever do it."

All that's silly and we all know that. Imagine if a baby had the same thought about walking: "I can't walk. I've never walked. I don't know why I even bother trying." It's silly, right? As adults, we do it with our goals, our dreams and our desires. So ask yourself, is it really going to be that difficult or is it going to be worth it? We need to stop putting obstacles in our way and start removing obstacles. Keep your eyes on the prize and the obstacles will fall by the wayside.

Take a look at the diagram above. Let's say the awesome little stick figure is you. You just graduated high school or college. You have this amazing dream and you're going to go for it, right? Whatever your dream is. Everyone's unique.

You graduate college and you say, "Yeah! I'm going to go for it." Then you go get a job. Now you have this time obligation. You now have to get insurance because you have to get a car. You've got to pay taxes. And you buy a house and you've got student loans and have to think about retirement, and the list doesn't end there, does it?

Now all of a sudden it's really hard for you to see your dreams. It's hard to be clear with that. What most people do is they will shrink their dream to match their paycheck. Disastrous! Terrible, terrible. Shrinking your dreams to match your paychecks is what 99 percent of the population does. Since you are here, reading this, I know you want to be in the top 1 percent and what I intend to do is expand the 1 percent into 2 percent. If we could double that, we would literally change the face of this country, so that's what my team and I are working toward.

"To each there comes in their lifetime a special moment when they are figuratively tapped on the shoulder and offered the chance to do a very special thing, unique to them and fitted to their talents. What a tragedy if that moment finds them unprepared or unqualified for that which could have been their finest hour."

~ Winston Churchill ~

Shrinking your dreams to match your paycheck is never going to help you.

- It won't help your family

- It won't help your neighborhood or community

- It won't help anyone you want to add value to

Shrinking your dream to match your paycheck is the worst thing you can do to achieve your dream.

Instead, what I would encourage you to do, is make your dream so big you can see past your obstacles...and then something magical happens - All your obstacles shrink compared to your dream! That's really what we need to be doing.

No more shrinking!

Living Within Your Means

You've heard the saying, "Live within your means," right? Good advice, right? I agree. However, people often hear it as scarcity. They think about cutting, budgeting, scrimping, saving, the rice and beans diet kind of thing. They are not experiencing anything good in life in order to afford groceries and pay off credit cards.

For most of the population, this is a good idea. We certainly don't want people claiming bankruptcy every ten years so they can get into more debt and repeat the cycle. For the majority of Americans who won't take responsibility for their lives, and the lives of their families, this is good advice.

"It always seems impossible until it's done."
- Nelson Mandela

A Different Interpretation

For you, and the millions of other people reading this book, "Living within your means" has a different interpretation. The best way—and the easiest way—to live within your means is to expand your means.

Make more money. Become more valuable. Help more people.

That's how you live within your means. It's not about shrinking. Especially when inflation is going up, taxes are going up and interest rates are going up. Shrinking to live within your means simply doesn't make sense.

Expand Your Means

Expanding your means is how you're going to live within your means. It's what making your dream as big as possible is all about! This type of expansion will create space in your life so you can experience your dream and your life's purpose.

The expansion starts when you get outside your comfort zone. If you always stay inside your comfort zone, you will never experience the bliss you're looking for. You won't experience the financial freedom or the healthy relationships you crave because your comfort zone is too small.

As soon as you expand it, you've created space for more things to start entering your life.

"Courage is what it takes to stand up and speak; courage is also what it takes to sit down and listen."
~ Winston Churchill ~

That's how it all starts, expanding your dream. Make it big. Make it bigger. And lastly, make it even bigger. It must be something that will intimidate you when it comes out of your mouth when you tell people. You're almost shocked to say it. That's how big it needs to be. It needs to be so big when people are congratulating you and telling you good job on the things you're doing, it's only the small stuff because you're working on such a big thing they can't even see it. They don't even know!

It's got to be a big dream. It's got to intimidate you. Don't let fear run you. It starts with desire. Obstacles show up. Expand your dream. And smash those obstacles.

Take back your existence or die like a punk!

CHEAT CODE #2
POWER UP: START A BUSINESS

"I'm not a businessman. I'm a business, man!"
- Jay Z

People ask me all the time, isn't starting a business risky? News flash! You are already a business. The only challenge is, right now you're operating as an employee. But as an American, you were born as a business.

What I mean is, you have every potential and every ability to grow, expand and start earning a profit. What happens instead is, we get talked into earning a wage. I think parents mistakenly say, "Let's teach this kid some responsibility and make them get a job." It doesn't teach them responsibility. It teaches them conformity and wage slavery. If you really want to teach someone responsibility, have them start a business. Help them start a business, and operate it, and grow it. That's how you learn responsibility.

I was taught about seven years ago profits are better than wages. Profits make you a fortune, while wages only make you a living. The truth is, in an average working life as a W-2 wage earner, most people are going to make between $900,000 and $1.1 million in a 35-40 year working career.

How does anyone working a job expect to get ahead in this world??? In the last three years, I've earned over half what most people will earn in their lifetime! In the next year, I intend to earn double what 99 percent of this country's population earns in a lifetime. So when it comes to jobs, if you're still not convinced, I've come up with a list of pros and cons for your convenience.

Cons:

1. The Boss

You have to put up with a boss. Even if you like your boss, your boss has a boss, and his or her boss has a boss, and he or she has a boss, who has a boss, who has a boss, who has a boss. And the bosses always have to come down on the next person in line. In Corporate America they say "shit rolls downhill." Whether they like to or not, it happens.

Putting up with other people's commands, for me and for a lot of people, is really frustrating. Especially when you're at the ground level and you're the one dealing with the issue or problem first hand. They're removed from it. But they're the boss. I also heard a long time ago, the reason you don't like your boss is because boss backwards is double [S]-S-O-B. The first S I've nominated as Super—the rest you get.

2. Traffic

Every once in a while I will set an appointment with someone where I end up having to drive in traffic. It blows my mind how many people deal with that kind of stress and agony on a daily basis! For the longest time I forgot what it was like to sit in traffic. It drives me crazy!

There are people everywhere and they're all trying to switch lanes. No matter what, we're all still going as slow as a bunch of giant tortoises in some thick mud, and just getting angry along the way. And these people aren't even getting paid while they're sitting in the stop-and-go madness! Traffic is terrible, not to mention dangerous. Did you know the majority of accidents happen within a mile of your house or place of work? It's because people are traveling to and from those two locations at least once each day. It increases the likelihood of an accident.

When I was nearing the end of having my jobs, I finally had a car and would just deal with traffic. Sometimes it would take me an hour to get to work in the morning. Everyone else was driving at the same time. But by the time I got out of work, everyone else was asleep or home, I could get home in 20 minutes. Most people just listen to music on the radio during their drive, instead of working to better themselves with audio books and classes. It's no surprise a lot of people in California drive nice cars. They spend more time in traffic than at home, and they want to be comfortable. They are spending more time in their car than spent at home awake. Isn't that crazy?

"Intelligence without ambition is a bird without wings."
- Salvador Dali

3. Taxes

W-2 is the most expensive form of taxation. Mistakenly, people think having a job and a steady paycheck is security. It's a false sense of security. It comes from seeing a regular paycheck. People think it's always going to be there and will continue month after month. They become super dependent.

It creates a dependency on the job and on the system. When you are dependent upon it, you can be abused. They can start demanding that you work more hours. They can start to add more stuff to what you are doing and not pay for it. All because of the feeling of dependency. Everything around your life is structured to match the paycheck.

Also, with the dependency factor of thinking a check is going to come every month, you get trapped into monthly payments for cars, electronics, and furniture. You think you can afford it on a monthly basis because of the amount the job gives you. That's a trap! It makes you buy mortgages without ever counting the cost.

4. Golden Handcuffs

The Golden Handcuffs come in the form of "Benefits" like health insurance, 401k Company match programs, PTO, etc. This is where you might think, "I would go start my own business, but the insurance benefits are amazing. So I'm just going to put up with this giant list of stuff I hate about my job, just to get this one other thing."

The genius idea behind Golden Handcuffs is they look nice. They're shiny and valuable and pretty. They look good and that's what draws people in. When in reality, you are still trapped.

You can have your own insurance in your own business as the owner. Using insurance as an excuse is just silly. You're just making assumptions without even looking into it. You can get your own insurance. Consider the price: your life dedicated to a company that does not have your best interests in mind, or a slightly higher insurance premium. Do the math.

That's where we go into counting the cost. If you have the Golden Handcuffs, you may pay less to have an insurance policy. But if you have your own business, you're paying much less in taxes. First, you're going to create savings there. Second, remember when we talked originally about how profits are better than wages? If you think it's expensive, then expand your business and make more money!

Study more. Bring on a new resource or a partner. Expand and when you make more money in your business (because when you have a business you have more potential to make more money) it will then minimize the cost of the insurance. If you just have a job, it's fixed income. They can manipulate the prices all they want and you can work way harder in your job. It doesn't necessarily mean they're going to pay you more.

With your business, if you pour it on, you could literally double your income in a short period of time. Then the cost of the insurance doesn't weigh so much and it's not a big effect on you. It's also the same idea when we talk about health, organic foods, pesticide-free foods in Chapter 5. People say "Well, it's too expensive." In the long haul, the damage you're doing to your body is the most expensive. So here we're going to be talking about health, vision and dental insurance coming from your employer. It's a mindset to put you into scarcity.

When they have you as a dependent, when you are relying on them for the job and insurance, you don't expand. First, you don't learn much. You don't investigate. Second, it kills your creativity and your mind. You just turn into a robot. I'm sure you have felt like this at one point in your job. How many times have you woken up a little late, missed your coffee and drudged through the day until the clock indicated it was the end of your shift? Cool, you have health insurance, but now you're a robot. Congratulations?

Years go by. Decades go by. Whoop-dee-doo for you. You had your insurance, but are you living the life you want? Are you experiencing life to its fullest potential? Are you getting paid what you're worth? Stop using the Golden Handcuffs and the insurance as a reason to stay at the job.

5. At Will

Do you know what "at will" means? It means they can fire you for any reason whatsoever. They don't need a reason. They can just fire you, let you go at will. Bye, you're gone and now what? Now you need to go play the game and try to get another job again. At will creates a highly competitive culture.

Think about the people who have their resumes posted all over the internet. For many, there is a line at the door for an interview. There's just so many people competing for jobs. If you have a business, you're going to be collaborating with people. In this scenario, you're not competing. Remember this: It's crowded at the bottom.

6. You are an Expense to the Company Where You Work

If the company has an issue with profits, they cut expenses. You're just a human resource to the employer and you're treated as such. I interpret this very literally. You are a human *resource* — not a *human* to your employer. You are not viewed as having human-life value. Since you may be cut at any moment in time, how can you honestly see it as security? Is this the peace of mind you need?

You have a false sense of security when the company can cut you at any time. Even if they don't release you, they can cut your hourly wage or the number of hours you work. I've seen this happen to people with families, bills and obligations! Either situation sucks because they may need every single dollar to get any enjoyment from their life. Now even a weekly dinner and movie is out of range for them.

With a job, your ability to add value to the marketplace is stifled. Actually, to be more accurate, the job environment of a job makes both being creative and working hard bad things. None of your co-workers want to look bad. So when you work harder than them, they will get upset. It's the mindset of a job. It's not the mindset of the business world. In business, we get excited to see someone doing better than us. It gives us a mark to hit and inspires new, innovative ideas. In business, we strive to be our best selves and create value using our unique skills.

7. No Time Freedom

In truth, nobody is in control of their time. Time simply passes. What matters is what we do with time. 99% of Americans have been tricked into believing their time doesn't even belong to them. They are "given" vacation days, sick days, maternity leave, etc.

One of my business partners told me about his previous job. He had 1000 employees and 3 personal secretaries. From everything you could see, he looked like a very successful person. He told me every vacation for 10 years was either canceled or cut short because of that job. So even when people get personal time off in their employment package, they get sucked right back in. They have no lifestyle or time freedom.

Some people will say they only work 40 hours a week. Okay, let's break it down by the hour:
- 8 hours a day of work
- 30-60 minutes for lunch
- 30-60 minutes for the drive there and back
- 30-60 minutes getting ready in the morning
- It can easily be a total of 11-12 hours a day, while you are getting paid for the 8 hours you are "on the clock."

The extra 2-3 hours eats into your family activities, hobbies, and even your sleep. It's going to prevent you from building strong relationships with the people you love. It could even cost you your health. And it's all for the almighty dollar.
At this point, many start justifying and say, "Well, what am I supposed to do? What do you expect? This is all they pay. I got to put in extra hours." We aren't even counting the bandwidth cost of the job occupying your mind when you are away from the job. When you're at home thinking about all the work still needing to

be done and the ridiculous politics in the office or job site. Your mind is still at work, even though your body is at home.

8. No Respect

As I interview people who have recently switched to entrepreneurship after having a job, I ask them why. One of the biggest reason is they didn't get the respect they felt they deserved. Their work was full of people yelling at them, putting them down, making them be here and there to do one thing or another—simple tasks that don't merit your time.

When I was working at the j-o-b, one of the things driving me crazy was I didn't get to pick my own bathroom breaks. I'd be working on a car when nature called, but the boss demanded that I get back on the floor. He insisted I needed to finish the oil change before I could go to the bathroom. Are you kidding me? What country am I in? This is America and I can't even go to take a leak without getting yelled at or judged or piss people off? It drove me crazy!

One of my first jobs was in a movie theater. I always worked holidays. I also worked at a restaurant open both Christmas and New Year, so I worked the holidays too. When my mom moved to a different state to expand her career, means and influence, I wanted to visit her. When I asked for time off, I knew I would miss out on money. Travel was hard and it has always been a dream of mine to travel the world. When a business owner takes time off, the business still operates and still produces. If you set it up correctly and operate under the correct foundation and principles, it'll actually operate better when you're not there.

"Try not to be a man of success, but rather to be a man of value."
- Albert Einstein

9. Little to No Pay Increase

You don't have any real control over your raise. The biggest downside is every day, every month and every year the cost of goods and services go up. It's called inflation. If inflation is going up 5, 6, 7 percent a year and the job gives you a 3 percent raise, it doesn't even keep up with inflation.

At my last job they offered me a $0.10 per hour raise. I was making $13 an hour. Let's do some quick math. An increase of a dime per hour is a .7 percent increase. Point seven. Inflation was 7 percent, so they were offering me 10 percent of the inflation rate. The raises are out of context for the cost of living.

When I had my first job, a junior bacon cheeseburger at Wendy's was $0.99. Now the price is $1.49, an increased price of 50 percent. During a training the speaker said I could double my income with a 3 percent raise over 18 years. Of course, it was a joke. Doubling your income is going to come from starting a business and gaining control over your investments. It doesn't get any better if you get a second job. The cons are just doubled. Don't get another job, let's start a business. Profits are better than wages.

"Action is the foundational key to all success."
- Pablo Picasso

When I worked at Jiffy Lube, there was a guy who had been there for 10 years when I started. He was making the same kind of money I was making and he was twice my age. If you don't have strong mental fortitude, you sink into the status quo and become like the people around you.

The status quo is poison. I remember the guy saying, "Well, you know, that's what they give you. You just have to figure out how to live off of it." It wasn't productive thinking. If you don't stand guard at the door of your mind this type of poisonous negativity starts to seep in. They just moan and complain about everything. They complain about the boss, the weather, the pay, the work itself and everything. The negativity starts to ruin your mind and what is going on in your psyche.

Many people get fooled by their 401k. They look at it going up every month. They never question if it is going up because the investment had grown or if it went up because of the money they put into it. When they are asked about it, it makes them mad to because they have been putting money into the 401k for years, only to realize it was going up because of their contributions. In many cases, most of the spectacular employer match and "growth" is eaten up by fees the brokers take and dips in the market. Why not put the money in a different project? Put money into paying off your house or car. Maybe pay for your kids to go to a better school or buy better food for your family.

"Life opens up opportunities to you, and you either take them or you stay afraid of taking them."
- Jim Carrey

Remember the bathroom predicament I mentioned earlier? When I started my part-time business on the side, it became a really big problem for me. I had to deal with agents, contractors, banks, title companies and mortgage companies. Since they do regular business hours and I was working 7am to 10pm, it was impossible to meet with them and difficult to even communicate.

I had to do my new business by phone and email. My boss wouldn't let me walk around talking on the phone all the time, so I would take "bathroom breaks" a lot. In the bathroom I would respond to texts and emails and talk on the phone with contractors who needed to look at the property to make sure everything was good before we closed on it.

These were critical conversations, but when my boss wouldn't even let me go to the bathroom when I wanted, how could I make the necessary phone calls? I got to the point where I rebelled "I've got to go to the bathroom, man, get out of my face." Sometimes, if the call got too long, the boss would knock on the door and ask what I was doing. I would quickly wrap up the call and make up an excuse, "Hey, sorry man, someone called me while I was in there. I just hurried up and answered their call."

The boss started checking my pockets and told me not to take my phone into the bathroom. I ended up hiding my phone in my sock. I had to make business decisions not employee decisions. It frustrated me that my W2 job didn't respect me enough to let me make a phone call. It felt like they were thinking, *Hey, you're our bitch. You're on our payroll. You do what we say. You have no life outside of here.* I wondered what if these business decisions I budgeted time for actually had to do with my wife and an emergency? What if I needed to check in with my kids a couple of times a day? It became clearer that this lifestyle got too much for what it offered —and it's not worth the paycheck.

I'll tell you what's really worth it—going through the struggle of learning new skills and wrapping your head around what needs to be done in business. You can make phone calls whenever you want. Go to the bathroom whenever you want. Take as many vacations as you want.

Not only do they demand you follow the rules while you're on a W2, they suppress any sort of personal growth for you. They hate their jobs as much as you and instead of saying "go for it", they make you feel like you're doing something wrong when you try to better your life. Your co-workers, boss and 95 percent of the people you see every day want to keep you in a bubble.

It reminds me of the crabs in the bucket philosophy. When you catch crabs and put one in a pot, it will climb out. When you put two crabs in you don't even need a lid, because as soon as one starts to climb out, the other one will just grab it and pull it down. When you have a bunch of crabs in a bucket and the same crab keeps trying to climb out, the other crabs will rip it to death. The crab dies because he wanted out.

Does it sound familiar? Does it sound like a job where they think if you want to get out they will simply fire you? You are trying to better yourself, pay off your bills and experience life. They're trying to kill it. It's incredibly disrespectful. If you accept this, you're going to settle for mediocrity. You're going to settle for less than you deserve, less than you are worth.

Some of my friends have four or five kids and they are struggling with the same income they had when single. Now they're working harder and the job doesn't give them a bonus for having kids. In fact, compared to the rest of the world, American employers give moms the least amount of time off when they have a baby. Other countries give six months to a year paid maternity leave. Here in America, it can be as little as ten days before they are expected to come back to work. They can lose their jobs or not get paid.

When people complain about business, they are usually people with jobs inside a business. They don't like the arrangement and they are not really complaining about the business itself. If they started a business, they would have time freedom and flexibility. They would have residual and passive income, tax write offs and the ability to include their family in the business. The family would be included and would help the business expand. It also teaches the family responsibility.

People who are stuck in a job complain a lot. Complaining actually just perpetuates the problem. We talk about the Law of Attraction. The Law shows the more you complain, the more you're going to get what you complain about. What you think about, you bring about.

Why Start a Business

We've been covering this incredible list of why a job sucks. Now let's go over why owning a business is so great. First, when a business is built correctly, you will experience time freedom and money freedom. Really what it means is you have choices. You get to choose how to spend your time and you have choices how to spend your money.

"Small opportunities are often the beginning of great enterprises."
- Demosthenes

Why start a business? Growth opportunities! Jim Rohn would say, "When you set a goal for a million dollars, the benefit isn't necessarily the million dollars. The real benefit is what the goal will make of you to achieve it." If you achieve it, you could give the money away and still be a millionaire because you figured out how to do it. When you have a business, you learn more about yourself than ever before.

Another great reason to start a business is control. You have control over where the company is going, what it's selling, the company policy, even the name of the company. You can pass it on to your children and generations to come. When you die, you don't get to pass on your job to your children. Would you really want to? With a business, there's a legacy involved. This plays into teaching responsibility to your kids. Instead of telling them to get a job and work in someone else's business, why not have your own?

If you have a job and really like it, a business gives you something to fall back on. It gives you leverage with your job. Just think if you didn't need the paycheck. Do you think you would stick to your own standards more often and sacrifice less when your employer demands more of your time? It also accelerates your retirement. At the end of the day, we don't need a pile of money to retire. We need a stream of money to retire and a business produces streams of income.

Growth Opportunity

There's growth in learning about yourself, but there's also growth in multiplying your income. In a matter of five years, I went from making about $575 a week to $10,000 a week. There is no way it could have happened with a job.

The biggest advantage is the tax write-offs. As a W-2 employee, you can get about 15 tax write-offs. As a business owner and real estate investor, you get more than 450 tax write-offs. It helps to think of it as a tax matrix. If you've seen the movie *The Matrix*, two worlds exist simultaneously. In one world, 99 percent of humans are plugged into a system. They don't understand what's going on and deal only with what's being fed to them. The main character discovers some people are unplugged from the system and they see it for what it really is. The system is manipulated to the advantage of the 99 percent.

The same thing applies here. There's the poor mentality and the wealthy mentality. I talk about this comparison a lot in this book. I'd like to make it clear what the differences between the poor and wealthy are:

- It's not about where you were born, your education level, family status or whether you had a functional family.
- It doesn't have anything to do with race, gender, spiritual beliefs, sexual orientation or gender identity.
- It has nothing to do with whether you wear glasses, have long hair or if you can touch your toes.

The only difference between the poor and wealthy people is what they put in their mind on a daily basis and how they decide to use it. That's it. That is the only difference.

I'm going to continue to draw this distinction because a lot of people think it is about the school they attended, what kind of car they drive, what kind of shoes they wear, what their friends called them in high school, their age, the type of nose they have or if they are left or right-handed. They just come up with the weirdest stuff.

It's none of those things. It's what they put in their mind on a daily basis and what they decide to do with what they have learned.

Let's talk about two people earning $100,000.

- The wealthy person gets paid with an EIN (Employer Identification Number.) The poor person gets paid with a SSN (Social Security Number.)

- When you are getting paid with a SSN, you get a W-2 and 33 percent of your paycheck goes to the government for income tax. Before you even get to touch your money, a third of it is gone.

- Wealthy folks have their business revenue come into the business and none of it gets taken away in taxes—zero. The wealthy business owner gets to use 100 percent of the money up front. You don't have an IRS agent waiting at the title company when you fix and flip a home, waiting to take a third of it. When you go to your mailbox to pick up the rent check, no one is waiting there to take a third. You can utilize 100 percent of your money.

Consumption versus Production

Corporations get our money in restaurants, entertainment places, amusement parks, going to stores, buying supplies, clothing and other kinds of stuff. In a poor person's mind, all they're interested in doing with their money is consuming. The money leaves their pocket and they spend it to consume. Even the vacations, the airfare, the golf passes and all of it go into just spending in the poor mindset. They just want all the stuff, the bright, shiny big-screen TV or boat to keep up with the Jones's. They fail to realize the Jones's are trying to keep up with them and are about to claim bankruptcy.

With a wealthy mindset, you spend the same amount of money, only you spend it to *produce*. When the wealthy spend money, they make sure that money will come back with friends. They will also get reimbursed from the government because the money is being spent on the business. When they go to a nice restaurant, they take a client or associate with them and have a conversation about creating more value. Guess who their business partners are? Usually friends and family.

They also employ their children and get a write-off to pay the kids and let the kids buy their own toothpaste, clothes, and school supplies. Ultimately they're spending money to build relationships, which in turn, will build the business.

- We have a conversation about the wealthy mentality mindset
- We will have lunch and spend 20 bucks on it
- Because we have a productive conversation about our business, we will write it off
- During the meal, we spend 20 bucks, but we have a hundred thousand or even a million dollar idea
- We act on the idea, create a plan to implement and profit from it
- We did spend money, but unlike the typical consumer who spends money to spend, we spend money to grow our business—Big Difference!

Let's talk about buying a new laptop. The poor mentality person is just buying a laptop to play games, watch movies, do email and surf the web. A wealthy mindset person gets the laptop for production and they communicate with business partners, create advertising and learn how to increase their income. The same money is leaving their pockets, but because the wealthy person is spending it on production, the government will reimburse them on their tax debt for this spending. On the outside, the purchase may look the same, but there is a big mentality difference. The intent is the difference. What's your intention?

Life Tax

This spending is unavoidable. It's part of playing the game of being in America. When you buy a car, you must get it insured before you can use it. You also have to pay registration and state tax, and this money simply leaves your pocket. We're going to call it life tax. Life tax is about 10 percent of your earnings, and the life tax applies to both the wealthy and the poor.

Let's look at what is left over after any automatic deduction from the government and the life tax. For the poor person it is 7 percent and for the wealthy person it is 40 percent. Taxes for the wealthy person occur *AFTER* they spend money. Wealthy people understand the game (just like the unplugged person from *The Matrix*.) They use the system to their advantage instead of being spoon fed the idea 33 percent is to be paid to the government immediately.

The wealthy pay tax with the 40 percent and a great strategy. After all the business expenses and other write-offs, they typically pay anywhere from 8-10 percent in taxes. So, in the end, the business owners have around 30 percent left over. With the 23 percent more money, they accomplish things like taking a family vacation, paying down debt, building up the business, giving more to charity and much more. The impact business owners make n the world is multiplied three times. How exciting is that?

With this understanding, I hope you are inspired to go out and start a business. The easiest business to start is buying rental property. You get tax write-offs, someone else is paying your mortgage, you receive cash flow and when the market goes up, so does the value of the property. You get appreciation which can be converted into cash later on. Many times the rental unit might be losing money on paper, but the cash is flowing with all those tax write-offs. With the proper business structure, you can get 450 write-offs by owning a rental property. Below, is an illustration of what we've discussed in the previous few paragraphs.

Tax Matrix

	Income Tax	Banks & Corporations	Life Tax	Left over
Poor	33% (SSN)	50% Consumption – Spending money to spend money	10%	7%
Wealthy	0% (EIN)	50% Production – Cost incurred in the production of income = Tax write-off	10%	40% Savings, Investing, Charity, etc

If you feel like you're paying too much in taxes, it's probably because of how you are getting paid. When you start a business on the side and make your first dollar, all the write-offs in your business count toward the W2 income you earn. So, don't feel like you have to quit your job and stop the job income before you're ready to make the switch to full-time investor. You can start taking advantage of this strategy TODAY!

It doesn't take a lot of brains to start a business. What it takes is the wisdom to make the decision, some confidence and a desire for change. Don't be a victim in the tax matrix. Unplug yourself.

You can make the switch! I am your cheerleader. I am your advocate. I am almost begging you to make the switch for your own good and for the economy's good. The more entrepreneurs we have, the more problem-solving people we have, the more access to capital. The faster money flows in this capitalist society, the more problems get solved. The more innovations we make, the stronger we stay as a community and as a country. It is important you start your own business.

Stop paying taxes before you pay your bills and lifestyle. Pay your bills first, and then pay your taxes. Once I learned this, it was so easy, and exciting for me to start my business.

Two Parts of My Business

My business has two parts. The first is solving real estate problems, which people will always have in America. While you're reading this book, someone is destroying a house. There is a dog crapping in a house somewhere, termites are eating another, a leaky roof is allowing water in and mold is destroying the property. It's happening all over the country right now. Angry tenants are putting holes in walls. Homeowners are losing their jobs and cannot pay their mortgages anymore. Couples are getting divorced and they have to get rid of the house. Elderly folks are dying and their children need to find a solution for the property. Families are moving and have to sell their house to buy a new one.

There are so many challenges that come up in life and that's where an investor, like me, steps in. I bring the solution to their problems. When I learned I could get paid to simply solve problems in real estate, I hit the books and enrolled in training programs to learn about the problems. I started learning what humans were experiencing and how to help them out of those problems. In the end, I provide a solution for a profit. But the focus was not on the profit, the focus was on the people and creating solutions for them. Profit follows solutions. If you chase profits, you are missing the point.

The other part of my business is sales and recruiting. It has been exciting to be with a real estate education company that paid me for bringing new students on board. It has been a business in and of itself. This was on a very part time/spare time basis. When I say I started the second business, I just mean I started talking to customers to look for solutions I could provide.

Every month, I'd put the money I was saving in taxes toward advertising. It may have been only a couple hundred dollars, but the small amount of money meant massive change in my business. It allowed me to find more customers to serve. When I got a customer on a real estate deal, I could make $20,000 profit. On a sales and recruiting call, I could make $10,000 profit. Either way, by spending time in those businesses, just a couple of transactions replaced my entire yearly income working two soul-sucking jobs. It's going to be the same for many of you reading this book.

When I started learning more about running a business, I started to see people would work harder on themselves than they did on their business. They were cleaning up errors in judgment. When you're a business owner, you can't go around blaming the boss anymore. You are the boss. When you stop blaming and you start taking responsibility, something switches in your mind. When you take responsibility, you empower yourself to take action toward your goals and aspirations. When you take responsibility, you *can* do something about it, and you *will* do something about it and you improve it.

Changed Mindset

As I continued to hang out with those business owners and saw people make in a month what I used to make in a year, changes started taking place. It was because they focused on something else.

Jobs make you think you get paid for time. Which is a false premise —you do not get paid for your time. You're told they will pay you so many dollars per hour. At first I was thinking I got paid $2,000 a month and working 40 hours. If I wanted to make $20,000 a month, I would have to work 400 hours a week. That is impossible because there is only 168 hours in a week, including Sunday. The equation doesn't make sense. We don't get paid for time. We get paid for value. More specifically, we get paid for the *value* we put into the time.

When I learned people were making $10,000, $20,000 or even $30,000 a week because they put that much value into the marketplace, I got really excited. In any job, it's hard to put that kind of value into the marketplace. It's a trap because it's a dollar-per-hour scale. Even if you did put the value in the job, they're not going to pay you for it because you've agreed to accept a certain number of dollars per hour, month, or year.

Now, there's a thing called the law of compensation. No value-added is ever lost. But in the moment you're not being directly compensated for it. So it becomes frustrating and discouraging. When you have a business and the right contracts and agreements in place, you are immediately compensated for the value you bring. We get paid for the *value* we bring.

"If you don't design your own life plan, chances are you'll fall into someone else's plan. And guess what they have planned for you? Not much."
- Jim Rohn

Raise Your Value to the Marketplace

How can we raise our value to the marketplace. First, you can develop more valuable *skills*. You can take classes to learn new skills. You can hire a coach to help you through the process and you can read books. You can also develop a more valuable personality. Andrew Carnegie, one of the richest men on the planet during his time, had a net worth of $400 million. He had Charles Schwab on his payroll and paid him $75,000 a year, which, in the 1900's was equivalent to just over $1.8 million in today's market. In addition to the $75,000 for his skills, he got an annual bonus for his personality of $1 million, which would be somewhere around $24 million today.

He got this $1 million bonus yearly because of his attitude and his personality. His job needed his $75,000 skill set. Andrew Carnegie recognized what Schwab was doing for the factory and the corporation was worth more. The personality Schwab brought and the way he helped raise everyone up was worth $1 million. Carnegie paid the $1 million gladly to encourage him to stay instead of go somewhere else.

My first year in business was tough because I thought it was just skills. I thought it was only about finding the customer, telling the story and building for an event. The event could be a video, brochure, valuable training or 1-on-1 lunch. At the end of the event, I followed up with the customer and asked for the order. I would go through the skill set, but wouldn't bring my personality into it. At the time, I didn't realize how important it is to be likable. Fortunately, the skill set pays, but the personality pays so much more.

The personality is the multiplier. We don't want to add to our income. We want to multiply our income by 5, 10 or 20. I started working on myself by reading more books and asking other people about my personality and character flaws. It was tough at the beginning to listen to other people's feedback on why I was an asshole. People would say I wasn't nice, I wasn't caring, I wasn't passionate. I was just going through the motions.

The skill part of the business is very technical and could be done robotically. I was so caught up in mastering the motions and neglected to bring any personality to it. I would try to beat people with intellect and logic instead of just making someone feel important. It was a big personality flaw and it was costing me tens of thousands of dollars each month. I would see other people making it big and we were in the same business. I just wasn't getting it. This went on for a little over two and a half years.

Ultimately I had to figure out what I was really selling. First, and before anything else, I was selling me and the idea that working with me would be beneficial to them, as customers. On the real estate side, with the real estate solutions company, the value I bring is peace of mind. I help people keep their home, avoid foreclosure and keep their tax bill low. That's part of it. The other thing I bring is financial solutions. Some people would have temporary financing on a property and couldn't get long-term financing. If they didn't fix that, they would lose their property.

Value in Teaching Others

Teaching people about what's possible is another value I bring to others. It's true on the sales side, education side, and the recruiting side. It all leads to peace of mind. The exact value I experienced is what I now help others experience. I'm bringing value to their life with real estate education and retirement account strategies. Helping people learn how to become financially independent is the most incredible opportunity in the country. I get a thrill out of teaching, even if it's just simple truth, like the basic principle of understanding profits are better than wages.

True Sample Scenario

A lady called us in response to a sign she saw on the side of the road. It read, "I'll buy your house. I'll make your payments." She called and one of my students answered. This woman needed help ASAP:

- She had a mortgage of $147,000 and was about to lose the house.
- If she lost it through foreclosure and it went to auction, the lender would potentially lose on the total balance of the mortgage and would have the right to sue, get a judgment, or a lien against the woman.
- Even if the mortgage company did not pursue her, the difference between what is owed and the amount the mortgage company got at the auction is considered income and the IRS wants to be paid taxes on it.
- She wasn't only concerned about her credit, she also knew the difference could easily be $10-20, or even 30 thousand dollars.
- The student who got the call needed a new place to live.

57

- He lived in a bad part of town with crack heads stealing from him and drunk people walking into his house—criminal activity happened on a daily basis in this part of town.
- His family was expanding with a new baby on the way and he didn't have the room or tolerance for this kind of risk.
- On top of it all, he's still paying 33 percent in taxes while working two terrible jobs on opposite sides of town. He was in a bad situation.

A major part of running a successful real estate business is understanding relationships. In our local community of investors we found someone with a retirement account getting a 0% annual return. We negotiated with him to create a win-win scenario all around. We borrowed $6,000. It covered both the $3,000 in late payments and $2,000 for us to repair damages. The investor was put in second position on the house, so now his money is collateralized.

- The basement had flooded with damage half way up the walls.
- Lead paint was peeling off and the asbestos ceilings were sagging.
- There were a lot of safety issues in this house and it was another reason why the woman needed to get out of the house—it was not safe.
- We gave her the remaining $1,000 for travel expenses to go home to California where she had a job waiting.
  This is impressive because our student had zero money and terrible credit. He worked two jobs and was in the same

position as I was about a year before. I knew exactly what he was going through. After working 20-hour days, he'd come to the house and fix it up so he and his family could move into it.

He now can take over the mortgage of $147,000 and a second position lien for $6,000. The basement had a separate entrance, two bedrooms, a bathroom and kitchen. He lived upstairs in the three bedrooms, two bath main house and rented out the basement apartment. He's responsible for the $1,000 per month mortgage. How much did he get for the rented apartment? $1,000 per month!

This completely changed his living situation. He went from hating how he lived and paying someone else's mortgage as a renter, to living on a corner lot, across the street from a church, while his tenants pay for the debt service on the home. At first, he used his increased cash flow to pay the investor off on the second lien. Once the investor was paid, the thousand dollars of rent started going toward making extra payments on the house. The baby expenses weren't such a big deal anymore. Even with a second baby, he was in a much better position with a nice fenced yard for the kids.

Not to mention, since the basement was a rental, he built a business qualifying him for write-offs. In addition, he had a better place to live, payed less in taxes and payed less for his house every month. His out-of-pocket expense drizzled to a mere $137 for a $147,000 house in an appreciating market.

When people tell me they can't do real estate investing because they don't have money—I genuinely laugh. All I have to do is point to this example and the excuse is gone. $137 is couch cushion money. If you can't pull the money together yourself, could you ask 7 friends for $20? If you can do that that, the next step is investing in real estate.

Best Time to Invest

It's common for people to ask, "Michael, when is the best time to invest in real estate?" The answer is simple. The best time was 20 years ago because we could have been riding this appreciation wave the whole time. The second best time is right now. This parallels with an ancient Chinese proverb, "When is the best time to plant a tree? Twenty years ago because you would now be experiencing the shade and the fruits of the tree. The second best time to plant a tree is now." Take advantage of the opportunity to add more value to the world right now. Otherwise in 20 years you'll be kicking yourself in the pants because real estate will have doubled in price, and taxes will have substantially increased.

Take back your existence or die like a punk.

CHEAT CODE #3

MULTIPLY YOUR INCOME

"The question isn't who is going to let me; it's who is going to stop me."
-Ayn Rand

Do you want to be wealthy? Then simply adding to your income will not be enough. You have to *multiply* your income. Don't you want to double your income this year and double it again next year and every year after? I have been building my own business, working with other entrepreneurs and mentors, over the last six years, and my income has doubled or tripled every single year. It keeps going up. Part of the reason is I have surrounded myself with professionals.

Upgrade Your Professionals

One important professional to upgrade is your CPA. Some people will say, *"I couldn't possibly fire John. He's a family friend who has been doing my accounting for years."* Okay fine, but if they don't have a wealthy mindset, why would you listen to their advice? If they won't make the adjustments you ask them to do, why would you continue to work with them?

You must surround yourself with a powerful team of professionals. The more they communicate with each other, the better it will be for you. Build relationships with your CPA, tax attorney, business attorney, insurance agents, etc. Some people might claim these professionals cost too much. The simple truth is, as a business owner you will need to pay for these things. If you think hiring competent professionals is expensive, try hiring incompetent professionals to save money and see where it gets you.

I am totally fine paying an attorney to figure out how to protect me and my business to keep me out of trouble. My job is to collect the money and I am very good at what I do. Their job is to keep me protected, and competent professionals do that very well. In addition to having a great CPA and attorneys, you will want to add real estate agents, title companies and insurance professionals to your power team.

The most important members of your power team are your mentors. These are people who have been where you want to go. Surrounding yourself with these people will give you many more ideas to multiply your income.

Stop the Blame Game

People will often blame the company they're working for keeping them in a state of poverty. We talked about this mindset near the beginning of this book. Never blame, justify or complain. It's really your own ideas and your own misapplied efforts that are holding you back. If you continue to work in someone else's business, you're just going to work for that dollar-per-hour and build their dream.

It's their baby. They imagined it. They brought it into reality. And they sold you on the idea to work for it. They're off somewhere goofing around, having fun, enjoying life, discovering all the benefits coming from being a business owner. You're stuck there working 50 weeks a year. You may get two weeks of vacation. But that's a big MAYBE.

How long do you want to be on that side of the equation? The reason those people are so successful is because as business owners, they can step away from their business and it will still work because they have a system. They have a power team to support them. They have all these people to watch their back, help them find the next deal and get them on the right track.

While their businesses may operate without them, any savvy business owner understands that his or her success is directly related to the thoughts and actions they engage with, and they assume full responsibility for any results produced by their business, good or bad. Some may shy away from responsibility, but that is the most disempowering move you could make in business, and life in general. If you don't want to take responsibility for the failures, you don't get to take responsibility for the successes. Step into an empowered state and start taking full responsibility for everything in your life. When you own it, you can change it!

Be a Source of Solutions

Your power team is going to be one of the biggest keys to multiplying your income. Again, upgrade your professionals. A wonderful thing about having your power team of professionals is they don't come to you with problems. They come to you with solutions. All these people are solution oriented. Remember, just because they hold a title doesn't mean they are worthy of your association. Make sure you understand their mentality.

You want to know their philosophy on business and know they're not socialists. Socialists in this kind of profession will not work for your business. You need hard-core capitalists to propel your business forward. They need to know how and why capital and economics work. Business only works because you're exchanging value. Capitalists understand this.

"Winners are not afraid of losing. But losers are. Failure is part of the process of success. People who avoid failure also avoid success."
- Robert Kiyosaki

Get in Front of People

Woody Woodward taught me there are three different ways to get an audience:

- Buy an audience
- Build an audience
- Borrow an audience

Which do you think is best? The answer is to borrow an audience. Building an audience involves a lot of hard work and time, buying an audience doesn't always work because you don't know where they came from. How do you do borrow an audience? The first step is to find someone in your niche who already has an established audience, someone with influence. Then, create or offer them something of value. The point is to give something of value without expecting direct compensation. If you want to multiply your income, the fast, easy and most effective way is to borrow an audience. It's one of the best marketing strategies.

Claim Your Authority

"Why should I listen to you?" You're probably thinking it right now. Here's what I tell people. I am one of the nation's best when it comes to sales, leadership, and financial strategies. I'm a product of the product I sell and I get it. I understand it. I eat, sleep, and breathe this belief. In a sense, I *am* the product I sell. This is how I make my business grow.

When I claim my authority, some people are taken aback. They think, *Wow, okay. I guess I'd better follow you. You've got some authority.*

You have to claim your authority. Nobody knows who you are until you tell them. You must talk yourself up, even though it may feel weird. If you don't show your belief in yourself, how can you expect anyone else to believe in you? If you say, *"But I don't have any authority. I'm not the best in anything,"* I won't believe you. You don't have to be the *best* in anything to claim your authority. You just have to put yourself out there with competence, confidence, and conviction. If you don't believe in yourself, then how can you expect anyone else to believe in you?

One of the easiest ways to claim your authority is to be a CEO. When you start your own business you are the CEO, so claim it. Show up as a CEO. Ask yourself how a CEO acts and works. How do they conduct themselves? What kind of professionals are they surrounded by? When you claim your authority it not only helps with your positioning in business dealings, it also helps your self-image. You really are the CEO of a million-dollar business if you have the resolve and mental fortitude to see it through. The more you introduce yourself as CEO of your business, the closer you will come to experiencing it firsthand.

Toastmasters International

Toastmasters International is an organization made up of people committed to becoming better public speakers. You may have amazing ideas and be well versed in the English language, but if you never learn how to articulate these ideas, you'll never be able to fully claim your authority. Not only will you learn from other members, but meetings are a perfect opportunity to borrow an audience. Pitch your business idea and see if you get any bites. Even if you don't, you'll get valuable feedback to apply to subsequent pitches.

Keep in mind the importance of adding value. Don't drone on about the features of your business. Give examples as to how your business helps your target audience. Give them a sample of the pepperoni on the pizza before you try to sell them the whole pie. When you give these valuable pieces for free, the audience will perceive the value of what you are sharing. Giving value requires you to understand the value of your audience's time. Your goal in any form of public speaking is to provide *more* value to your audience than they would have otherwise gotten within the timeframe. Your audience invests valuable time in you - make it worth their while.

> *"Fastest way from start to money is your warm market."*
> *-Bob Snyder*

Networking Events

Networking events are an excellent place to meet other professionals and potential clients. The sad thing is most people misuse their time at networking events. They take a "law of averages" approach and focus on giving their business card to as many people as possible. The theory is they will meet someone worth their time as a byproduct of exposing themselves to as many people as possible. You are much better off finding one or two people you have an interest in and getting to know them on a deeper level.

We *remember* the people we meet and form a deep connection with. What is the use of collecting 100 business cards if you'll forget about these people a week after the networking event? The next step is to decide whether the initial connection is worth another meeting. It is often in this second meeting where you get the "feel" of what it would be like to work with a person.

Understanding Scalability

Once you grow your business to a certain level, your essential question to answer becomes "is *my business scalable?*"

- Can you take your current business systems and duplicate them in another city?
- Is there a way for people to take what you've created and run with it?
- Can you step away from the business and have it still operate?

Can your business be duplicated? People will watch you and you want to think about the things you want them to duplicate. If you don't want 100 people doing something, like placing a higher priority on money over the people, don't do it yourself. If people benefit from doing it exactly as you have done, continue to do it and others will follow you. Duplication is one of the fastest ways to scale and multiply your income.

Cash-flow Banking

The strategy is to slightly over-fund a life insurance policy to build its cash value. Most policies have a guaranteed rate of growth. They grow at a fixed percentage regardless of the stock market. Over time, you will build up enough cash value to cover your monthly premiums. At any point you can borrow against the cash value of your policy.

Let's say you built up the cash value of your life insurance to $100,000. This money is going to be earning a guaranteed rate of return year after year. When you want to go get a car it costs $25,000, instead of going to Bank X and giving them 6 percent on an auto loan, you can get a loan from your own policy at 5 percent. Not only will you get a better interest rate, but you're policy is still earning the guaranteed rate on the $100,000. The $25,000 loan you took does not affect interest you earn, making this a much better option than borrowing from a 401k.

You have to get your cash value to a point where it at least covers your monthly or yearly premiums in order to take full advantage of this strategy. Let's go back to the example above. If you use this strategy, you don't have to pay off your entire loan. If you stop paying, the amount is just subtracted from your death benefit. No harm to your credit, no harm to your cash flow, no harm to your way of life.

Now imagine if you get the auto loan and miss a couple of payments. Next thing you know your car is repossessed and your credit is ruined. Even if you pay back the full $25,000, the bank ends up making thousands in interest. The first scenario allows you to pay back a loan from your insurance policy in full, then the $25,000 simply goes back into your policy and is available to you for the next car, home, emergency, hardship, etc.

I recently had a conversation with a friend who had just purchased a commercial warehouse space, and he had gotten the loan from his life insurance policy. The best part? It was a life insurance policy his mom had set up for him as a kid! Life insurance policies create flexibility with funding. When an opportunity comes up, you can multiply your income because you have some funding from the life insurance.

When you put yourself in this financial situation, then you

will attract more opportunities than the average person. Think about it. To get a business loan from a bank requires you to basically sell them on your idea. They can always say no if they don't believe in your idea. This insurance policy strategy puts *you* in complete control.

We're just scratching the surface on multiplying your income. It's going to blow your mind. It's easy to get into early retirement mode when you use the right strategies from owning your own business. You can start putting money into different investment vehicles that start to spin off cash for you—life insurance, real estate, investing into yourself and your education. Multiplying your income is a lot easier than you think. It comes down to the relationships you build with others and knowing how to get in front of (borrowed) audiences. Speaking of retirement, let's cover how to use retirement accounts to multiply your income.

Retirement Accounts

"I never dreamed about success. I worked for it."
-Estée Lauder

How wealthy people view retirement accounts differs from how regular people view retirement accounts. We are taught to focus on building a large pile of money, and then to live off this pile of money for the rest of our lives. I really want to point out a few discrepancies and look at some numbers.

We graduate college around age 22 and work until around age 65. We work for between 40 and 45 years, and we are supposed to put a portion of our monthly income into our retirement accounts. The goal is to build up a big pile of money. We save for years and years, decades and decades. Let's look at what this looks like in reality.

Say you want to live off $3,000 a month when you retire. In order to be retired for 20 years, you would have to save $1,040,000. What happens if you live into your 80s or 90s? What are you going to do in those extra years? You are out of money. What's interesting is financial planners, Wall Street and other financial institutions suggest you put aside a million dollars.

But guess what? The average American only earns $1 million over their entire working career. Let's look at some statistics on how education affects lifetime earning potential.

- Those with a high school diploma earn an average of $900,000.
- Those with an Associate's degree earn an average of $1.1 million.
- Those with a Bachelor's degree earn an average of $1.8 million.

To save $1 million, someone with a Bachelor's degree would have to live off $20,000 per year, *before* taxes! The national poverty level for a family of 5 is just under $29,000 per year. After doing this math with me, you might be feeling discouraged at this point. How is one supposed to save a million dollars when they don't even make $2 million over their career? And I'm reeling with laughter at this point —isn't it ridiculous? You *aren't* supposed to. It's not part of the system.

Saving your way to retirement is a myth. We were taken away from pensions and put into retirement plans like a 401(k). They gave us slightly more control of our own money, but we've had tens of millions of people go through this and very few have any money left over. It's a big challenge, right?

What if you're like most Americans, and you don't think you could live off $3,000 per month? Realistically with inflation year after year, $3,000 simply won't cut it, so let's say you go for $5,000 per month. To get paid every month in 20 years of retirement you'll need to save $1.7 million. If you want to get $10,000 a month, you will need $3.4 million saved up. Less than 1 percent of people living in the Unites States earn that amount of money in their entire lifetime, even less *save* that amount of money.

Remember banks are in the business of cash flow, but they tell you to build up a pile of cash. Then, all of the sudden when you go into retirement, it's time to switch your strategy and live off the cash flow. For decades, all we've been trained to do is build piles of money and the situation becomes intimidating and dangerous. It's a challenge for everyone, especially when taxes or interest rates go up. The cash flow from your pile of money could be worthless.

Right now, the median amount the average American has in their retirement account is $3,000. By retirement age, which is 65, the median amount in a retirement account is $12,000, which means they have been saving for decades and only have $9,000 more than the average American. I want you to be critically thinking. People are so wrapped up in employer matching plans. Well, whoop-dee-do. If you're in debt on your car or house and are more concerned with putting money into your retirement, you're done. It's not going to work. We need to run our lives as if we are businesses. Simply put, it's money in vs. money out. What return are the funds in your retirement and savings accounts putting into your pocket on a monthly/yearly basis? Is it enough to cover the monthly/yearly cost you're paying to the banks and corporations for your car loans, mortgages, and lifestyle? That's where your return needs to be. Do the math.

You are fighting an uphill battle with stacked odds. You need a better retirement strategy. I wrote this book so you can avoid these mistakes and not fall into the potholes that get millions of Americans stuck, and if they get out, in new debt. You don't want to think you are going to save your way to retirement. It's not about piles of money. It's about streams of income. If you don't know about the rule of 72, it's important you understand how it works. Using the rule of 72, you can easily determine how well your money is working for you. Take the number 72 and divide by the investment's rate of return to learn how many years it will take for your investment to double. See example below.

Qualified Plans & 401 (k)

When you signed up for a Qualified Plan (QP) you may not have read the fine print notifying you these are government controlled. With the government controlling the accounts, if they decide they need the money, they can take it. And you agreed when you opened the account.

$$\frac{ROI}{72} = \text{Years it will take for your \$ to double}$$

Checking _____ $72/.01 = 7200$ years

Saving _____ $72/.11 = 655$ years

Money Market _____ $72/1 = 72$ years

CD _____ $72/2.05 = 35$ years

} You will die before your money doubles!

Asset-based lending

Long Term

$72/8 = 9$ years

Short Term

Private $$
$72/12 = 6$ years

Hard $$
$72/18 = 4$ years

Sure, you get a tax write off for contributing to your 401(k), but is it worth allowing the government to control your wealth? There are some qualifiers limiting your contribution too.

First off, you can only put earned income into your 401(k). Passive income like rent checks, royalties, or dividends cannot be invested into a 401(k). You are also limited to a maximum of $18,000 in contributions each year. Even when you're earning more than $100,000 a year, you are still limited. That's all you get to put in the account. When you retire the government takes their cut of your savings in taxes. They consider the money you get at retirement to be a taxed distribution. You work all those years to grow your wealth, and a sizable chunk is taken away before you get to spend one penny.

The worst thing about taxed distributions is you have no idea what the tax rate will be by the time you retire. Income tax today is between 30 and 40 percent. Sure, taxes could be lower by the time you retire. On the other hand, they could be *much higher.* Are you really willing to gamble with your retirement money like that?

I know *you* care about the future tax rate, because *you* aren't average. Unfortunately, the average American simply doesn't care about taxes. They only care about taxes in the context of how much money they get for their annual tax return. If you care about how much money you'll pay the government, then a 401(k) isn't the best account for you. Jim Rohn, one of my mentors, said:

If the company or government is in charge of your retirement account, you can plan on dividing your account total by five. If you are in charge of your retirement account, you can multiply your account total by five.

The security of a 401(k) account is another misconception held by many Americans. They are more stable compared to riskier investment accounts, but these accounts are still tied to the stock market. Think about how many times the stock market has significantly dipped in the last 20 years.

Here's a list:

- October 1997 Mini-Crash – Rattled by Asia's currency crisis, the Dow Jones Industrial Average plummets 554 points for its biggest point loss ever. Trading on US stock markets is suspended.
- March 2000 Dotcom Crash – A historic economic bubble and period of excessive speculation, a period of extreme

growth in the usage and adaptation of the internet by businesses and consumers.

- September 2001 – Following the worst terrorist attract in U.S. History on Sept. 11, the market plummeted on its first day of trading after the American Stock Exchange and New York Stock Exchange had been shut down for almost a week.

- October 2002 – After recovering from lows reached following the Sept 11 attacks, the market dramatically declined in July and September leading to lows last reached in '97 and '98.

- October 2007 – Mainly due to poor lending practices, the market became inflated, hitting unsustainable highs. This record-breaking crash is likely to be the one that comes to mind first when you hear the words, "stock market crash." This was the beginning of a terrible mudslide of hungry and homeless families.

- September 2008 – By this time, the market had declined by 20%. It was not until March 2009, having lost 54% or its value since October 2007, that the market rebounded.

- May 2010 – Short-lived, this Flash Crash was a trillion-dollar stock market crash that lasted 36 minutes.

- August 2011 – A sharp drop in stock market prices due to fears of contagion of the European sovereign debt crisis to Spain and Italy.

- August 2015 – Wall Street suffered a major starting loss as the Dow opened 1,000 points down.

- June 2016 – Investors in worldwide stock markets lost more than the equivalent of 2 trillion dollars, making it the worst single day loss in history.

Reading this information, it is plainly obvious that smart people like us have little to no control over when and how hard the stock market will crash. Learning from history and seeing these 10 dips in 20 years, we can estimate that there will be 15 to 20 dips in the market over a 40-year career. Someone is making profit from your loss. You know who ultimately profits from these dips and rebounds? Financial institutions.

Say you have a $100,000 investment. The market dips and your investment loses 50 percent of its value. Your financial institution then builds this investment back up to $75,000. They will frame this as 50 percent growth. While this is technically 50 percent growth on $50,000, you're still down 25 percent from your original investment.

This process happens with every subsequent dip in the market. It may seem like you gain with each rebound, but in reality, you're lucky if you get back up to your original investment. Sounds frustrating, right? This is my issue with 401(k)s and qualified plans in general.

IRAs

The IRA, which stands for Individual Retirement Arrangement, is another type of qualified plan. Here are some of the qualifications of an IRA:

- Contribution is capped at $5,500 a year for those under 50 years of age.
- Contribution is capped at $6,500 a year for those over 50 years of age.
- Contribution is on pre-tax money.

We have talked about the actual taxes on retirement accounts, but we haven't talked about the *hidden* taxes. What do I mean? Fees! Kathy Kristof of the *LA Times* wrote an article recently about how these fees are eating up over half of the average American's retirement savings.

The study in the *LA Times* focused on $1.8 trillion in retirement money invested in mutual funds. The average saver contributes $4,000 annually to their IRAs of this 1.8 trillion in assets, 2 percent goes to fees to pay financial planners and fund managers. This works out to roughly $2,180 in fees per account. If the average American only contributes $4,000, they pay an average of 54 percent in fees! Understand the fees are lethal. The fees vary depending on the account and amount contributed, but in general, higher funding equals higher fees. That is pretty sad. They are a hidden tax most people have no idea they're paying. Referring back to the business mindset of money in vs money out, is your return on your money large enough to cover these fees as well?

The system is flawed. Up until a Supreme Court ruling a couple of years ago, brokers didn't legally have to disclose all of their fees. Now they have to disclose their fees upfront. Many financial institutions have since reduced their fees, but they are still outrageous.

Count the cost. Please, count the cost and take a real look at what you're doing with your money. Pay attention to who sold you the plan you are currently working and find out who benefits from that plan.

Featured in Kathy Kristof's article is chief executive Mitch Tuchman, who estimated a 35-year old who puts $4,000 in IRAs each year will lose roughly $1.1 million to fees by the time they withdraw their money at 76. Why? Because fund managers make their money from keeping their client's money in the market. Is the market up? Fund managers will advise you to invest more to capitalize on the boom. Is the market stagnant or spiraling? Fund managers will advise you to invest more in order to position yourself for the boom around the corner.

These financial professionals make their money off of average people. Like I said before, *you* aren't average. After we cover Roth Accounts I'm going to show you how to multiply your income with self-directed retirement accounts.

Roth Accounts

There are several types of Roth accounts, with the Roth IRA being the most popular. The caps of $5,500 and $6,500 are the same as any IRA. You invest with after-tax funds, but they grow tax-free. When you get your money at retirement, it's tax-free. The analogy is, do you want to pay tax on the seed, or do you want to pay tax on the harvest? With the Roth IRA, you pay taxes on the seed, so the harvest is tax-free. The growth is tax-free as well. They're still qualified plans, but their fees are still going to kill you.

These funds are tied to the stock market in bonds and mutual funds. If the market goes down, so does your retirement. You didn't do anything different, but it feels as if you are being punished. Why are you investing this way? Who sold you on this plan? If your money was invested in bank notes, seller finance notes, tax liens or rental properties, they are not affected by the fluctuations of the stock market. You chose to invest in financial vehicles designed to give cash flow.

> *"Go ahead and switch the style up. And if they hate, then let them hate, and watch the money pileup"*
> *-Lloyd Banks*

The Solution: Self-Directed Retirement Plans

Here are some sobering statistics for retirement-aged Americans, according to the U.S. Bureau of Labor Statistics:

- 20 percent of Americans 65 and older are still in the workforce.
- This rate has been steadily increasing since 1995 and is at the highest rate ever.
- 60 percent of U.S. households have no money in a retirement account.

So, what's the solution?

We've talked a lot about the problem. The solution is not piles of money. Instead, the solution is self-directed retirement plans. With self-directed retirement plans, you are in total control of your money. You are the investor. You are the shot-caller who decides how to grow your retirement account.

The IRS doesn't describe where a self-directed IRA invests. They simply tell you that you cannot invest in one. The IRS forbids these accounts from investing in:

- S-Corporations (only people can invest in an S-Corporation)
- Life Insurance Policies
- Collectibles (Coins, Stamps, Gems, Artwork, and Antiques)

Anything else is fair game. Some of my personal favorites include:

- Storage Units
- Retirement Communities
- Movie theaters
- Restaurants
- Mobile Home Parks
- Single Family Homes
- Apartment Buildings
- Gas stations
- Car washes
- Vehicles

You can invest in businesses, seller financed notes and promissory notes. You can invest in tax liens, land and commercial operations. There are so many things you can invest in having nothing to do with the stock market. These are things you can control – things you can see and touch – things you can manipulate – things you can depreciate and get write offs just for owning them.

These are things you can insure and collateralize. If you want to start a business, you can use your retirement account to invest in it.

If you want to learn more about what you can do with a self-directed retirement account, then check out "The *Self-Directed IRA Handbook*", written by my friend Mat Sorensen. He's got a ton of information in that book. Here's an example: The first way of being a passive investor is to own a self directed retirement account. The next one will be about an active investor-owned self-directed retirement account.

Self-Directed Retirement Accounts in Action

As an example, let's say a friend has $400,000 in a self-directed retirement account. He wants to invest in real estate because he feels like he knows property better than he knows stocks and mutual funds. Real estate is insurable and free of hidden fees. Not to mention the tax benefits for property owners.

He followed the proper steps to unlock the money and roll it over to a self directed retirement account where his $400,000 is in a different account. Now, instead of the single digit returns from the stock market based retirement account, he has the opportunity to make millions.

He wants to be a passive investor in some real estate deals. After all, he knows about real estate and doesn't know about stocks, bonds and mutual funds. He knows he is sitting in real estate now or headed toward some, or just left some. Real estate is insurable and the tax benefits are incredible. He can write things off, depreciate the assets and it is unbeatable compared to the stock market.

"Men are what they think about all the time."
-Nate Lambert

Knowing the benefits of real estate, but not being an experienced real estate investor, he can still make a good investment. Let's say our team finds an amazing house we can fix and flip. I know how to do fix and flips and run projects efficiently enough so we can sell them and pull profit out.

We have an opportunity to purchase a property for $300,000 with the rehab on the property of $50,000. We need $350,000 to complete the deal. If we went to a regular bank, they wouldn't give us the money. Banks look at the cost to value benefit. They might give us 65-70 percent of the value of the property. In an as-is condition, we would be lucky to get $200,000 from the bank to buy it, leaving us needing another $100,000 to finish the purchase and $50,000 more for the rehab. Instead, we talk to the friend with a self-directed retirement account and create a deal.

We use all the proper documentation to determine amounts, terms, collateral, timelines, penalties, and "what-ifs". We use a title company and lawyer to put a stamp of approval on everything. Always use title companies. Always. When do we use title companies? Always!

It takes us six months to do the purchase and rehab. The promissory note says we will pay the friend a 12 percent rate of return. When most people are getting less than 4 percent in their retirement accounts and losing 54 percent of their earnings to fees, a

12 percent return is pretty strong. Add the fact the property is insurable, collateralized and gets great tax benefits, and it is even stronger.

- We sell the property six months later for $450,000.
- The 12 percent interest is the same as 1 percent a month.
- $350,000 x 1 percent is $3,500 interest per month.
- $3,500 x 6 months means $21,000 in interest which goes right back into his account.
- When the house is sold, agent fees and closing costs are another $26,000.
- Total payments for fees, interest, and principal are $396,000.
- The $54,000 profit goes to the private investor actively involved in the deal—you or me.

All funds, plus interest, are put back into our friend's self-directed retirement account. The trust deed promissory note is paid off and he has a $21,000 passive profit and it won't be taxed because it is going back into the retirement account. It's wonderful. If there is a lawsuit, the retirement account cannot be sued. The money is in there and it's protected. He made $21,000 in a six-month period of time while doing nothing and taking very little risk. If I didn't pay him back, he would get the property. He could rehab it himself, sell it and get the $54,000 too. Worst-case scenario, he makes more money! This is why people want to do self-directed retirement accounts.

Investor Pool Expands

When the friend who made $21,000 in six months starts talking to his friends, he tells them he used his self-directed account to get a 12 percent return, while the investment is insured and collateralized. His friends say, "What? Dude, I just lost 1 percent (or more.) What do I need to do to get that kind of return on my investments?" The friend who has already made good money now has the ability to start partnering up to do more deals or bigger deals.

- We're able to buy more and more property.
- We can start to buy and hold instead of doing fix and flips.
- The partnerships can last five, ten years or more.
- The tax benefits pass through to the investor and reduces tax liability.

Now let's look at a more active investment approach. We are also going to use real estate in this example. Say the friend's friend has a retirement account with $100,000. He rolls it over into a self-directed retirement account. He finds a property for $80,000 and has $20,000 left to fix it up. He sets up a title company and has his retirement account purchase the deed. The $20,000 goes into an escrow account to fund remodeling.

In this case, you are not allowed to do the rehab work yourself. Unfortunately, it is against the law for you to do your own remodeling on this type of investment. The law is to ensure the quality of home improvements within the fix-and-flip industry. Now, say our new real estate investor is able to sell this property for $150,000 after four months on the market. He pays $100,000 to his retirement account. Another $10,000 goes to agent fees and closing costs. He is left with $40,000 profit.

The rate of return in those four months is 40 percent. If he could do this three times a year, it offers a 120 percent return on a retirement account you control and has been collateralized. That's huge! Your goal is to get this type of return year-over-year to exponentially grow your income. Every year your money is doubling, doubling, doubling with the potential of growing your own self-directed retirement account to multi-millions.

Investing for Cash flow

If you want to continue to double your retirement account each year, you will have to do a lot more deals, or you could start investing for cash flow. A couple of years down the road and you'll have built it up to a couple hundred thousand dollars. And just like that you're ready to go buy an apartment building.

Say you find a 12-unit apartment building for $400,000. You direct your retirement account to purchase the property. If each unit rents for $1,000 a month, you're going to earn $12,000 a month in passive income.

Of course there are some operational expenses. You can figure 40 percent of this will go to operational expenses. Things like maintenance, property management fees, and advertising fees. You'll have about $7,200 a month in profit after these fees. Take $7,200 a month and multiply by 12 months and we're looking at $86,400 a year in profit.

When it's properly set up, the $7,200 a month is going in the self directed retirement account and the cash will flow as long as you own the property.

Do you want to be able to use this money before you retire? All you have to do is set up a 72(t)-early distribution. This gives you immediate access to your monthly cash flow. You can do whatever you want with this money. There's huge asset protection from the money being in your retirement plan. People cannot sue you and take the money. Someone may be able to get a judgment against you, but you don't own the property. Your retirement account owns it. Right? You are just the beneficiary of the retirement account.

You're the one who gets to take cash flow and invest in what you need to invest. It's your cash flow. You can use the money to live, you can donate it, you can do whatever. As long as you set aside the 40 percent we talked about for vacancies, maintenance, repairs and all, the property is going to produce and keep producing forever. Think about it. You turned your $400,000 lump sum into $86,400 of passive income every year, until either you sell the properties or real estate becomes unnecessary or irrelevant (not likely).

Passive income is also taxed differently. It can easily be transferred to another beneficiary who can inherit instead of letting it go into probate or letting the government try to take some of the money with a hefty inheritance tax. It simply gets moved into your beneficiary. It's so important you start designing these plans and stay really aware of what's going on.

Never forget, never take advice from brokers who are not truly interested in what actually happens. They are just there to collect their own check. With an educated, well-designed plan it's insured, collateralized and secured. You know what real estate is. You know what an apartment is. There may be a very small annual fee or transaction fee, but there are so many benefits to this strategy.

"Luck is a dividend of sweat. The more you sweat, the luckier you get."
- Ray Croc

Bank Funded Non-Recourse Loans

Some of you are going to start off with your first $20,000 - $40,000 property and you're going to let the cash flow go back in. Guess what? Banks will lend to your retirement accounts. If you have a self-directed retirement account, you can get what's called a non-recourse loan from the bank. They'll want some collateral and usually only lend up to 60-70 percent of the loan to value. So if you had $30,000 you could still buy a $100,000 property with your retirement plan because you can close the gap with the non-recourse loan.

Non-recourse means if you default, they can't sue you. They can't foreclose on you. Retirement accounts can only get non-recourse loans and it's good news for you. You begin to earn money and the cash is flowing. It's secure. Your asset protected. People can inherit the property from you when you pass without losing money to inheritance tax. It's probably the smartest strategy anyone can use —self-direct your retirement accounts.

Don't let your lack of knowledge hold you back. If you don't know real estate, or you aren't good at it then partner with someone who does and lend them the money to do the real estate related work. The example we used earlier for passive income was 12 percent, but it is just an example. You could lend your retirement money at 15 percent or more. At this point, you are the bank and you decide. If the investors or rehabbers don't like your terms, they can find someone else to partner with. You could even require the investor to have "skin in the game" to give you confidence about loaning them the money. It's all up to you. You invest in what you know and not what your employer is pushing you to invest in or what the stock broker thinks you should invest in. My mentor, Garrett Gunderson, says, *"The risk isn't in the investment. The risk is in the investor."* Get educated.

Take back your existence, or die like a punk.

Cheat Code #4
ANNIHILATE YOUR OPPONENTS

"Winning is a habit. Unfortunately, so is losing."
- Vince Lombardi

What you think you know about banking was taught to you by banks. Start asking more questions, especially from the banking and other financial institutions you interact with on a daily, weekly or monthly basis. What are their intentions? What are they doing? How does the whole thing work? Why do they offer certain products: Why do they say things in such a round-about way? What is it all about?

Earlier in the book we talked about the Rule of 72 and calculating your earnings with your checking account, savings and money market CDs and all. Now we're going to take it a bit further and start asking what these bank products actually do for us.

"Pain is inevitable. Suffering is optional."
- M. Kathleen Casey

Lines vs Loans

I want to highlight the difference between lines and loans. There's a very distinct difference between them.

We've all been told we shouldn't use credit cards. We are told they are bad and should only be used for emergencies. Think about where we heard it – the banks are the ones who promote the idea. Now, why do banks push people to take out loans? Well, it comes back to the differences between lines and loans. What are the benefits to the bank?

Loan: Your mortgage costs you $1,200 a month in debt service for a $200,000 mortgage at 6 percent interest.

Credit Card: You have a line of credit in the form of a credit card with a $15,000 limit. You've racked up the current balance to $12,000 with monthly payments of $600 at 21 percent interest.

The average American is paying $600 per month in credit card debt with a 21 percent interest rate, compared to the 6 percent rate on the mortgage. Which of these two would you think is the preferred lending instrument for the bank? Most people would say that 6 percent is lower than the aforementioned 21 percent, but let's look at a few more things.

Lines, like credit cards, are revolving. It is similar to a checking account because you put money in and money comes out. You put $1,000 in and the very next day you can pull the $1,000 back out. Its functionality is just like a checking account, except it is a line of credit. Your credit card's payment fluctuates based on the monthly balance; in fact, so does the effective interest rate, because it's recalculated on a daily basis rather than monthly.

A loan is one directional. You only put money in …and put money in … and put money in. You just keep putting money in. Also, because it's one directional, the payments on the loan can now be "amortized" which means you pay the same amount every month until the balance is paid off. Both are simple interest products, but the leverage of lines is much greater due to the power we have to affect the daily interest. We also retain fluidity of the principal we pay.

Now that we've established the differences, let's take it one step further. Let's look at your cash flow. Let's say you have a $5,000 monthly household income between you and your spouse. Most people will have at least two bank products for their money—a checking and a savings account. We'll get into checking accounts in a minute, but consider this question: What is the point of a savings account? How does it actually benefit us? If you want to become wealthy, follow what wealthy people do and it is not stockpiling their money in a savings account. If the wealthy don't have savings accounts, why are you using one?

RECAP TWO TYPES:

1. **One Side:** Amortized loans

   one-directional

2. **Other Side:** Simple-interest lines of credit

I have a couple of theories. While I am not a conspiracy theorist, I am an observer. I pay attention to what's going on. In terms of financial benefits, a savings account isn't anything. It doesn't pay the interest rates other investment vehicles pay. It's basically pointless.

As Americans, we think we're doing something right by saving. We put our money in the savings account because we feel it is important. And besides, we don't know where else to put it. If you look at the costs against the benefits, you might want to reconsider having a savings account.

Here's the Breakdown of a Sample Budget:

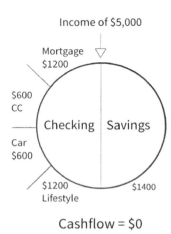

Income of $5,000

Mortgage $1200

$600 CC

Car $600

Checking | Savings

$1200 Lifestyle

$1400

Cashflow = $0

- $5,000 combined monthly income
- $1,200 mortgage payment
- $600 credit card payment
- $600 car payment
- $1,200 to cover the rest of our bills and lifestyle
- $1,400 for short-term and long-term savings which may include a retirement plan contribution and maybe the savings account at the bank

At the end of the month our cash flow equals zero. Zero, because we've allocated all the money and our entire income is gone.

Beyond Accumulation

The old philosophy is really forced on us by society. If you want to retire, you need to accumulate money. Accumulate… Accumulate…ad infinitum. But that doesn't work! Look around. It simply doesn't work! The people who are truly retiring are doing so off of steady cash flow, not off of a big pile of money saved somewhere.

Cash flow is King.

When you understand this, it will ultimately put you into a financial position you desire. Create and then live off the streams of unending cash flow—NOT a big pile of money that will eventually run out.

"If you don't understand interest, you pay it. If you do, you collect."
- Tony Scotty

Cash Flow Tools

Stay with me as I explain how you can change your mindset and immediately create cash flow. Our example shows the $5,000 per month income. Immediately go and put the entire $5,000 toward your line of credit (credit card.) Now your $12,000 balance is reduced to $7,000. Next start paying bills and expenses out of the line. YES, you can do that!

By doing this you get two immediate results. You have reduced your effective interest you pay because of the reduced balance and you now have cash flow. Because you paid $5,000 on the credit card, you no longer have the $600 monthly payment. Your cash flow is increased by $600.

What I want you to pay attention to is the fact that we're not sacrificing lifestyle by doing this. You okay with that? We're just changing the way we do it. There's no sacrifice here. Technically, you have to sacrifice your old mindset. But as far as your lifestyle goes, there's no sacrifice.

Let's carry this scenario further. We put our monthly $5,000 in and pay our $3,000 monthly expenses. In one month you go down $5,000 and then back up $3,000. The next month is the same, $5,000 in and $3,000 out. This pattern continues and think about how long it will take to pay off the debt. In this example we started with $12,000 in debt. With this method, we have $2,000 cash flow, so it's only going to take about six months to get the balance down to zero. Six months! That's it! Now, you've effectively paid off your credit card. If you followed the old way paying the minimum each month, it could be five, six or even seven years of paying 21 percent interest while you are financially strapped with no cash flow.

You can park your entire income on this line. It's called Velocity Banking because we start to really chunk it down. Those with a wealthy mindset understand. Those with the employee-mindset think of cash as currency and only use leverage in an emergency when the cash runs out. The wealthy individuals flip the idea on its head and utilize leverage as currency and cash as velocity to pay down their debts. As you saw in the credit card scenario above, it's a very effective strategy.

"The person with the most information wins."
- J. Massey

Your Mortgage Loan

In our example, we have a $200,000 mortgage with a payment of $1,200 per month. Let's understand what is really going on with the mortgage loan. Our payment is comprised of a ratio of interest and principal. In the first years, the ratio looks similar to this: Out of the $1,200 payment, $950 goes to interest and only $250 is going to principal.

You may say, "Wait a minute, I thought it was 6 percent." Well, yes, over the course of the year it actually is 6 percent of the actual principal, but the payment has been "amortized" to give you a predictable, "manageable" payment over the next 30 years. Consequently, your principal part of the payment is very small in the early years. There's an even bigger challenge with the issue—every five to seven years people tend to move. This time frame when you are paying the biggest portion of your payment to interest, not paying down your mortgage loan.

When people sell their house and buy a new one (or refinance their current mortgage to lower their payment) they are starting the amortization process all over again from ground zero. This traps them into a seemingly never-ending 5-7 year loop of paying most interest!

You'll find the other crazy thing when you look at your Truth-in-Lending statement in your loan documents, it will show you that making the minimum payment for 30 years will equal something like $420,000 you have paid on the $200,000 loan. Now, that's a lot of money, right?

To further illustrate just how insane this is, let's take a snapshot of your mortgage's amortization schedule over a 48-month period. Over those 48 months, we're going to pay down the principal by about $13,000 when making $1,200 payments at 6 percent. During the 48 months, you paid $44,000 in interest. It's simply NOT FAIR! We do it every day with our mortgages and passively accept it as the norm.

Home Refinance Game

People say, "Let's refinance and put the car in there." They ultimately stretch the debt out from 30 years to 35-40 years. You never get out of debt this way. You never get out of debt using those kinds of bank products. But they'll start sending you letters three to four years into the mortgage saying they can lower your payment by $100 a month—"Refinance Now"—you're tempted to say lowering the payment by $100 would be worth it. If you decide to go for it at the end of 4 years, you still start the amortization clock all the way over to Day 1. You effectively threw $44,000 of interest away for nothing. It's gone forever and to add insult to injury, you will pay around $3,000 in fees (hidden away snuggly in your new mortgage) to pay for the refinance process. Does the $100 per month seem worthwhile now? Count the cost.

Consider Ditching the Savings Account

Next, consider the $1,400 you are putting into savings. Before we go any further, let's point out something additional. If you need to buy a new car and are a typical American, you would continue to put the $1,400 into savings. Let's say you have built the account up to $10,000. Now, you need to buy the new SUV and it costs $10,000. Although you have the cash, you have been trained, "Don't touch the savings account."

The bank has instilled this way of thinking. So, we leave it alone. Why does the bank instill this way of thinking? Because in the banking world, they are authorized to lend to people based on how much they have in the savings pool. The bank combines your money with all the other savings accounts and lends to anyone who walks through their doors at a profit. Meanwhile, they pay you almost nothing for holding your money. Let's say they give you 1 percent because the math is easy.

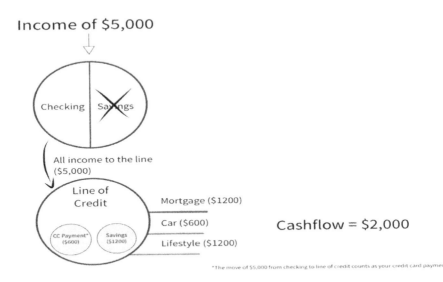

Income of $5,000

Then because you don't want to touch your "rainy day" fund, you go to your bank and get an auto loan for $10,000 to buy the SUV. They gladly extend you a loan with a 6 percent interest. Basically you gave the bank $10,000 and they gave you 1 percent interest. Then they charge you 6 percent to use your own money in the form of a loan. It appears to be a 5 percent gain for the bank, but it's not. It's a 500 percent return for the bank.

Think about it in dollars. If I sold you a marker for $6, that I bought for $1, I just made a 500 percent return on my money. That's what the bank is doing to you.

Instead of playing their game, use the $1,400 to pay on your line of credit and increase your cash flow. By not allocating the $1,400 to savings, we increase our cash flow again…this time by $1,400. Combined with the $600 freed up credit card payment, this amounts to $2,000 per month in cash flow. It's a simple matter of tweaking our mindset.

Now you say, "Hold on Michael! We need a "rainy day" fund. What happens if we have an emergency?" You are still "saving" the $1,400 every month. But you're holding it on your line and paying down your debt until you need it. You can see how this is much better than having the money sitting inactive and doing nothing in a savings account. If you have an emergency, you can still charge the expense to your line. You're protected.

Attack the Mortgage Next

Earlier in the book we talked about paying off your credit card (line of credit). What do you want to do next? Pay off the mortgage. Let's say you now write a check from your credit line for $13,000 as a principal only payment toward your mortgage. Your credit card is not right back up to $13,000. But remember, when you paid the mortgage the old way, the $13,000 was going to cost you

$44,000 over four years.

What's it going to cost you when you move the $13,000 onto your line? Here's the math. $13,000 at 21 percent interest is to be about $2,700 a year. Using the methods you have already learned, you'll be able to pay the $13,000 of in about 6 months. That's just $1,400 interest for half the year to pay off the same amount of principal instead of the $44,000 to pay off the mortgage loan. And it took only 6 months instead of 4 years. Then all you have to do is do it again.

"A person has to remember that the road to success is always under construction. You have to get that through your head. That it is not easy becoming successful."
- Steve Harvey

When you continue to pay down 48 months worth of principal this way every 6 months, you will pay off your $200,000, 30-year mortgage in 5-6 years and done it without getting a raise or changing your lifestyle. That is POWERFUL!

In addition to being out of debt, you also have freed up another $1,200 and added it to your cash flow because you no longer have a mortgage payment. You now have $3,200 per month in cash flow before practicing the Velocity Banking Strategy. The payoff curve steepens the more cash flow you free up. We start to pay debt off faster and faster. It accelerates everything: A LOT!

After You're Debt Free

You paid off your car. You paid off your mortgage. You paid off your credit cards. You have a new problem: you're out of debt.

I bet you never would have thought being out of debt would be considered a problem. Well, if your intent is to become wealthy, it definitely is. If you don't get more debt, you'll have to start accumulating money in a bank account. That's what poor people do. It's what W-2 employees are taught. What do wealthy people do? They buy ASSETS. You know have the opportunity to start using your newfound knowledge to acquire some properties.

$210,000 House for $187.32

People have property problems every day. They're getting divorced. They're facing foreclosure. Or maybe someone died. Maybe they need to sell quickly because of a job transfer or lost some income and need to reduce expenses. Maybe they just need to buy a new house because their family is expanding. These kinds of problems happen inside the real estate world. For some people, the only way to solve their problem is with the creativity of an investor.

Here is an example where a friend bought a house on the brink of foreclosure for less than $200. He got creative and took over someone's payment. The previous owner was backed into a corner and was about to lose the house altogether. My friend structured the deal so he could take over the existing mortgage payment of $1,000 per month and leave the financing in the previous owner's name. The property is a duplex and both units get $1,000 each or $2,000 per month total.

First we had to invest in improvements to get the full rent amount. We put in about $6,000 to do carpet, paint and fix a few plumbing issues. Once it was done, our cash flow is $1,000.

Remember, we owe $1,000 each month to pay off the $200,000 mortgage. With the cash flow, we can accelerate this.

Remember, my friend still had a full-time jobs and bringing in $5,000 every month. Personal expenses are now only $1,200 a month after paying off the personal debt. Our cash flow before buying this property was $3,800 per month and this new property produces an additional $1,000 in cash flow from the renters. With the increased cash flow and the $1,000 payment on the seller's mortgage, we are going to pay $5,800 a month to the principal of the mortgage each month. And you still don't have to get a raise or even had to change your lifestyle to do this. With our Velocity Banking Strategy, the duplex is paid off in about three years. Let it sink in for a minute.

"First they ignore you, then they laugh at you, then they fight you, then you win."
- Mahatma Gandhi

Out of Debt Again

You have this paid-for asset: the duplex. How do we keep the ball rolling? We go down to the bank and tell the banker we want a HELOC on the duplex. A HELOC is a Home Equity Line of Credit. Remember, we want lines. We don't want loans.

We get a $150,000 HELOC secured by the equity of the duplex and put it to work. We need about $15,000 each to acquire more properties on average. That would equate to put $15,000 down on 10 properties. 10 properties!

What do we want in minimum cash flow for each of the properties? I ask because, again, it doesn't matter how much comes in, it matters how much we get to keep after expenses. Let's just say each of the properties produces $400 in cash flow. (I recommend you don't buy property if they don't cash flow at least $400.) You will have vacancies, improvements and repairs you will have to spend money on, so you need the cash flow to cover them.

You've acquired 10 properties using your $150,000 HELOC. With each property generating an additional $400 each, you have $4,000 total per month—in cash flow. Now, we're a few years into the plan and you have developed skills, resource and the ability to do this using Velocity Banking. We're going to start paying down these properties in HUGE chunks.

Now, a few years later, you have 10 properties free and clear with an average rent of $1,000. With this example, you now have $10,000 per month coming in passively, no matter what. Wherever you are in the world, the $10,000 shows up. No matter how much you spend, the very next month another $10,000 shows back up in your life. At that point, do you really need your job anymore if you don't absolutely love it? This is the lifestyle. It's the way to be financially free.

It's not about building up big piles of money. One of the scariest things is thinking, "Okay, if I want to retire off of a pile of money, how much do I need?" It's the way Wall Street, banking institutions and the government wants you to think this way. They say fund your 401k, fund your IRA, sock away a big pile of money, then you can live off the interest. Sounds ideal, but if you do a survey across the county, you find less than 1 percent can actually do it. Right now, we have 78 million baby boomers in the United States and 55 million of them have less than $1,000 in their savings accounts.

This plan does not work. Instead, we NEED cash flow.

"Get up, stand up, Stand up for your rights. Get up, stand up,
Don't give up the fight."
- Bob Marley

Another amazing benefit of building wealth and passive income is the continued rise in income as rents go up over the years. You increase rent by 3 percent every year. It just goes up and up and up. As inflation goes up or taxes go up, the amount of rent you charge goes up too. Your lifestyle and your cost of living are covered and acceleration continues. Maybe you start buying apartment buildings. Before long, you're a member of the 1 percent club. When you are making this type of money, it's tempting to buy cars and other fun stuff. But if you buy property first, it will pay for your stuff. If you want a Mercedes CLK GTR, great! Buy an apartment building producing the cash flow for the Mercedes.

As a W-2 employee, we would have financed the car with hard-earned money, along with a bunch of interest. Instead, as an enlightened wealthy mindset, we set up the apartment building cash flow to pay for the car. The apartment tenants pay for it. The result: we get the car paid off in five years, AND we still have the cash flow produced by the apartment building. It's incredible!

I need you to be crucially thinking about this kind of stuff. Are you banking by default, or are you banking by design? You live your life by default or design. It's the same thing with your banking, your relationships, your health, and your family—all of it. Default or design. Which do you want?

When you critically think and design a banking flow it will

lead to true financial freedom. Now, when you pass on, the apartment building is in a trust, the car is in a trust, and your family gets to inherit it tax free. The government doesn't touch it. We'll talk more about trust and asset protection in the next chapter.

Pay attention.

Question the system.

Don't do life by default.

Design this stuff!

Take back your existence or die like a punk.

CHEAT CODE #5

REPLENISH YOUR HEALTH

"Health and cheerfulness mutually beget each other."
- Joseph Addison

Healthy Practices

What do you think when you hear healthcare?

Obamacare is probably on the tip of your tongue right now. Sadly, to the majority of the population, this means prescription drugs, harmful treatments, high premiums, etc. Guess what? You don't have to rely on the broken system!

Some people absolutely hate the healthcare system. To them, insurance companies and government regulations make it a broken system. Later in this chapter, we'll go over **health savings accounts (HSA)** and how to really maximize their potential so they can take care of you in your sickly days. We're going to use HSAs just like in the retirement accounts, except this time we're making your *own* healthcare system.

Health + Care

What does "healthcare" really mean?

Let's start by breaking it down. Health + Care. For me, and for most responsible people, this simply means taking care of your health. It starts with making healthy choices and keeping your body in prime condition so you don't have to make those doctor visits.

Now, of course, an annual exam is necessary for your health. Keep going to those visits. However, when it comes to taking medication for conditions that are self-inflicted, such as obesity and high cholesterol, we must take a look at how these issues came about. These conditions can be reversed and prevented through clean eating and exercise.

My mom is in the healthcare industry and works as a healthcare provider. She absolutely loves taking care of people, whether it is helping people maintain their health or rehabilitate their health. She has to offer help based on how she finds them.

One thing she often encounters is people making excuses about why they are eating the food they eat. It's no mystery America is fat. The problem is poor diet leads to poor body function, which leads to the mind not functioning correctly. The body stores the mind, and our mind comes up with our ideas, our tenacity, our thrills, and our love our adventure, creativity, inventions and our clarity. If the housing for our mind is in poor condition, the mind will also operate poorly. Hence, poverty.

People get stuck in a backwards loop. They say, "If I make more money, I'd buy better food. Then, if I buy better food, I'd feel better. If I could feel better, I'd do better and I could make more money so I could buy better food. I encourage you to start taking care of your body now. When you get mental clarity from taking care of your body, you'll be able to think better, work longer hours and feel more energetic. You'll sleep better and produce more. You'll make more money and it will be even easier to afford high quality foods. Then you just keep the progress going.

You don't stand in front of a fireplace and say, "I really want some warmth from the fireplace. As soon as it gives me warmth, I will put some fire wood in." The idea is silly. You've got to put the wood in first. Then it gives you warmth. The same thing is true about your health. You've got to start investing in quality foods. Eating in a healthful way will ultimately clean up your body, clean up your mind, give you better ideas, assist in launching you to be financially free in a matter of years, instead of hoping to retire in a couple of decades. We want you to excel. Part of living wealthy is living healthy.

Living Wealthy is Living Healthy

The art of living wealthy is living healthy. How do we clean up our errors in judgment? Jim Rohn said, *"It's an apple a day."*

Isn't that the truth! It's an apple a day. It is not seven apples on Sunday or thirty apples at the end of the month. It's an apple a day. It's about consistently eating good foods every single day.

Notice how the saying is *not* a Snickers a day, a cookie a day, a donut a day, or a cheeseburger a day. It's an apple a day. There's a lot to living healthy, but we're going to keep it simple and easy for now. This is a financial book based on numbers. So, let's talk about numbers.

Did you know there are numbers in our food? I'm not talking about, or necessarily promoting, calorie counting. Calorie counting is an okay gauge, but it's not all about calories in and calories out . . .

If it were, then we wouldn't have an obesity problem. Fair enough?

I really have to thank Ron Williams for his contribution into my health because of the knowledge he's gathered in the many years and decades of research and experimentation to create fantastic body transformations. I'm just going to share some of the basic knowledge I learned from Ron.

Let's look at the 80/20 principle:

20 Percent Effort - 80 Percent Results

We already know it's not a matter of calories in and calories out. The next thing to understand is the building blocks of food. First, we have carbs. There are two types of carbs, which are simple and complex. Next are fats. We have saturated fats, and then poly and mono unsaturated fats. Last is proteins. There is plant based, animal based, and dairy based proteins. Now let's get to the numbers in food.

"To keep the body in good health is a duty...
Otherwise we shall not be able to keep our mind strong and clear."
- Buddha

Numbers in Food

In order to create a happy body, we need to look at more numbers. What is your ideal body weight? I'm not here to tell you what it should or shouldn't be. Your weight is a personal preference at this point.

If your ideal body weight is 180 pounds, you look at this number and use it to calculate the amount of protein, carbs, and fat you need each day.

The equations are:

Protein*: (Desired Body Weight) x 0.6 = Daily grams of protein*

Carbs: *(Desired Body Weight) x 1.5 = Daily grams of carbohydrates*

Fats: *(Desired Body Weight) x 0.2 = Daily grams of fat*

Example:

Protein: *180 x 0.6 = 108g Protein*

Carbs: *180 x 1.5 = 270g Carbs*

Fats: *180 x 0.2 = 36g Fat*

Fats, carbs, and proteins are measured in grams. You want **0.6 grams of protein and 1.5 grams of carbohydrates per pound of ideal body weight a day**. If your goal is to weigh 180 pounds, then your target is about 270 grams of carbs per day.

These should be spread out over your entire day and not all in one meal. Same thing for your proteins. If you think about it in meals, it's about 30 to 40 grams of protein, per meal, and about 90 grams of carbs per meal.

That's easy, right? One food we really want to avoid is simple carbohydrates. Simple carbohydrates taste the best, but they create an unhealthy spike in insulin. These are things like chips, candy, donuts, cake, and similar sugary junk foods.

Simple carbohydrates send a message to your pancreas and squeeze a spike of insulin into your blood so that it can digest the carbohydrate. You get a big energy spike and it makes you feel good. Not much later, you get hungry again. You go eat a bag of chips and it spikes your insulin for another 30-60 minutes. After this spike comes a crash, and you end up hungrier and worse off than you were before you ate the simple carbohydrate. You don't have to completely cut out simple carbohydrates, but you do have to limit them to once or twice a month.

You can still indulge in chocolate or your favorite chips, but everything in moderation. Simple carbs are not something you go to for nutrition. Simple carbs ultimately lead to the creation of fat. They send a signal to the body that says it's starving, and this causes the body to convert the simple carbs into fat for later use.

That's what your body does. It's been evolving over thousands and millions of years and that is how it's evolved. Think about how you're communicating with your body. For your body food is language.

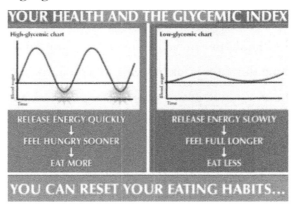

What signals are you sending your body? Are you taking coffee breaks and snack breaks throughout your day? Are you constantly spiking your insulin, only to have it crash again?? Wouldn't you like to have a lot of energy all day? The best way to do that is to focus on complex carbohydrates.

Complex carbohydrates are leafy greens and grains such as quinoa. Quinoa is one of the foods astronauts take up into outer space because it is a carb and protein combination. It's a complex carbohydrate and it has protein in it, so you don't get the spike of insulin. It stays level all day. You have this steady, slow, and even release of insulin into your blood.

When you eat a bag of chips, or a donut, a surge of insulin goes into your blood, but then it quickly goes away. Some examples of complex carbohydrates are:

- Leafy Greens (kale, spinach, lettuce)
- Avocados
- Steel Cut Oats
- Quinoa
- Brown Rice

Complex carbohydrates take many hours to digest, instead of 20 to 30 minutes like simple carbohydrates. This slow digestion supplies you with energy all the way until lunch. Then you have a great lunch and have energy all the way until dinner. If you eat right, then you'll never feel hungry between meals. If you feel hungry, you're doing it wrong.

"Good health is not something we can buy.
However, it can be an extremely valuable savings account."

- Anne Wilson Schaef

Fats

There are two categories of fats - unsaturated and saturated. There are then polyunsaturated fats and monounsaturated fats. These two are the good fats. We need good fat in our bodies. We *don't* need saturated fat. Saturated fat clogs your arteries. It's the fat you *see* on people. The challenge with fat is the same challenge you have with carbs. The saturated fat tastes good.

It's in foods like gravy, butter, popcorn, chicken nuggets, and cheeseburgers. They all taste good, but if that's all you eat then you're going to have a freaking heart attack! You can't always see it, but high saturated fat in your body is going to put you at risk of heart disease. It clogs your arteries and puts you at risk of a heart attack at any minute.

The American way is, "If I have a heart attack, or I'm having a failing heart or valve, I just go have surgery and fix it, a bypass surgery." Four years later and, since they didn't change their habits, they go in for another surgery. They usually don't survive their third heart attack. All because they couldn't give up saturated fat. It's so selfish.

Now, if you're healthy right now, you can have saturated fat in very small doses. The max is 10 to 15 grams of saturated fat per day. It's simply not worth exceeding this limit. It literally changes the way your body works.

Your gallbladder is constantly trying to process this fat and pull it out of the intestines and out of the blood. When your gallbladder gets overworked, it creates gallstones. Gallstones build up and eventually create a clog, which requires surgery to remove. Limit your saturated fat intake to keep your gallbladder healthy.

Poly and mono unsaturated fats are the good fats. They give us good cholesterol, and this good cholesterol keeps our skin healthy and our hair looking nice. If your mindset was to get healthy by cutting out *all* fats, then you'd actually be hurting yourself. The *right* fats are an essential part of a healthy body.

The following are great sources of poly and monounsaturated fats:

- Almonds
- Walnuts
- Pecans
- All Natural Peanut Butter
- Avocados
- Olive Oil
- Coconut Oil

Consider nuts to be all fat. This means you can't just go to town on as many almonds as you want. 25 to 30 almonds a day should be your max. Olive oil and coconut oil are much better than canola oil. Have you ever looked at the production of canola oil? The plant workers are in full hazmat gear and they put the oil up to 600 degrees, which creates carcinogens. It is not for human bodies at all!

If a recipe calls for canola oil, then use coconut or olive oil instead. Don't worry, coconut oil won't make your food taste like coconuts. Avocado oil is also great for cooking. Just be sure to never, ever use margarine. There's a reason most European countries have it banned. They don't consider it food, so it can't be sold or manufactured there.

"Rest when you're weary. Refresh and renew yourself, your body, your mind, your spirit. Then get back to work."
- Ralph Waldo Emerson

Even though America is the greatest country on the planet, the FDA and the USDA don't really have their act together. It's on you to really get educated on this. When you start to eat good fats, you don't feel hungry. You think, *Oh, its 5 o'clock, time to eat,* instead of, *Oh my God! I'm so hungry I can't even think anymore.*

This is *especially* important when you're at work and trying to be productive. If you're really hungry, your productivity goes down. It's bad for the economy, your paycheck, your company, and your reputation. Making this transition is going to improve so many areas of your life. There are plenty of places to get poly and monounsaturated fats without sacrificing taste. Now let's talk about proteins.

Protein

The biggest key with protein is lean, clean protein. When I say lean, aim for 7 percent fat content or less. If you go get ground beef or ground turkey and you're going to make your own burgers or meatloaf, then it has got to be lean.

Some of these packages of ground beef are up to 30 percent fat. Get the leaner version. You don't need the fat. I know some people say, "But fat makes it taste so good." Put some freaking pepper on it if you want to make it taste good. Use the proper herbs and spices. The fat isn't worth it.

When I say "clean" protein, I mean ask where it came from? Did the farmers who raised this meat use hormones? On a lot of farms, conditions are terrible and the animals get sick as a result. The farmers give these animals antibiotics to keep the livestock alive.

Think about the word antibiotic. You are a biotic. All living things are biotics. Taking antibiotics kills bacteria, but if you're constantly consuming antibiotics it can kill you too. You are constantly consuming antibiotics if you eat these animals from these farms. How do you think the cell production in these animals happened? It didn't happen in a healthy way. They were sick, but they kept them alive with antibiotics so they grow big enough to be killed and then sold to you as meat for your family. When animals are kept alive with antibiotics, how do you think the cell reproduction happens in their bodies? It didn't happen in a healthy way.

You need to discover where your food is coming from. You don't want to put those chemicals into your body. "Clean" also refers to what these animals eat. Was the chicken fed the grains, seeds, worms, and bugs it would eat naturally? Or was it fed leftover corn that has been processed and modified into feed?

I have a dog, and I don't feed my dog regular dog food because it's made of corn. Dogs don't naturally eat corn. If a dog was left on its own, it would never eat corn, yet 90 percent of much of the dog food is corn. When you look at the shelves and start reading the ingredients, you're going to be pissed off. When you get pissed off is when you make a change and commit to a better future.

Lean and clean protein doesn't just include meats. You do not have to be a carnivore to consume mass amounts of protein. The following are all great sources of plant-based protein:

- Beans
- Peas
- Quinoa
- Soy
- Steel-cut Oats
- Peanut Butter

If you decide to go vegetarian or vegan, just remember you've got to keep the soy in check. Soy should not be your main source of protein. Also, keep an eye on the sodium found in protein. The idea is to keep your sodium intake low.

Drinking Water

Number one on your priority list needs to be drinking enough water. There's something you need to know about water, though. Not all water is the same. Some municipalities pump fluoride and chloride into their water supply. They figure fluoride keeps people's teeth clean and chloride keeps the water clean. Bull crap. We really don't need this stuff in our water

Fluoride is intended for topical use. You put it on your teeth and brush it right off. It shouldn't be in your blood stream. Chloride cleans pools. Why would you want to drink it? You'd never drink pool water, yet these municipalities think its okay to put Chloride in your drinking water.

Avoid tap water. Using a Brita filter or something similar filters out stuff that breaks off in the pipes, but some of the stuff is infused in the water and gets past the filter. We want to look at water processed through reverse osmosis.

The cleanest water available is reverse osmosis water. You want to make sure that there are the electrolytes and minerals in the water you drink, because just plain H20 would actually clean out your body. You need the electrolytes and minerals. They create the electricity and dynamic that gives you good blood chemistry and muscle action. You are 70-plus percent water so don't drink junky water. It will ruin your body.

A good rule of thumb for drinking water is the 8x8 method. The 8x8 method states you should drink eight 8-ounce glasses of water per day.

"If we can get people to focus on fruits and vegetables and more healthy foods, we'll be better in terms of our healthcare situation."
- Tom Vilsack

Don't Abuse Your Body

Your pancreas and your gallbladder are incredibly powerful organs. They are processing units in your body, but they're very hard to replace. Pancreatic cancer is one of the deadliest cancers. It has a 1 to 2 percent survival rate, yet people abuse their pancreas like crazy.

They'll drink eight glasses of soda at a meal and abuse their pancreas, but then they're afraid of spending $100 on good quality food because they're so wrapped up in money. Just think about how many extra miles you are putting on your heart, pancreas, and gallbladder.

Treat your body like a Ferrari or Lamborghini. You wouldn't attach a trailer to it and start hauling around 5 tons of gravel, would you? You would put unnecessary wear and tear on your tires, transmission, engine, brakes, axles, and differentials. You'd be lucky if it lasted a year. It's going to break down or the cost of maintenance is going to completely outweigh the cost of the actual car.

This gravel is a metaphor for bad foods. A lot of times when you actually look at the label, it's not even food! It's what I call edible food-like product. You might as well be eating Play-Doh. It's non-toxic so you should eat it, right? You look at a box of cereal, it'll say things like "13 essential vitamins and minerals" and "heart healthy". Then you read the nutrition facts on the side of the box and see there is nothing healthy about it. 40 to 50 grams of sugar, which is a simple carbohydrate, in one serving? No wonder our kids are whacked out! They're addicted to this sugar and it messes with their energy levels. They struggle to concentrate. They don't sleep well. It sets them up for failure in life. They get diagnosed with ADD and ADHD. Then they're put on these freaking pills and the pills turn them into zombies. It's Sad.

Let's look at what is actually in the food you buy. Do not focus on the front of the box. Focus on the side and back of the box. Companies are not allowed to lie on the nutrition label, but they can manipulate you with unregulated marketing tactics on the front of the box.

It will have a stamp from the American Heart Association. It'll say, "The American Heart Association says 10 grams of fiber per serving is important. Well our cereal has 10 grams of fiber per serving so this is American Heart Association approved." Yet look on the side of the box and there's tons of other junk. Are you kidding me?

There's all this junk they put in our foods that isn't allowed in other countries, yet we're supposed to be the greatest country. It's okay to eat bad food every once in a while. If you go to a wedding and there's some cake and a cheeseburger, help yourself.

You're going to have over 1000 meals throughout the year. If 5 percent of your meals are "cheat" meals, it is only 50 to 70 meals. It works out to about 4 to 7 meals a month. Just save these cheat meals for special occasions. If you have friends coming into town, then go out to a nice restaurant and eat whatever you want. Just keep it balanced.

The more you are adamant about having a healthy body, the more your friends will be adamant too. You are the average of your four closest friends. If they're all fat you're going to be fat. If they're all fit, you'll be fit. If they're all sad, you'll be sad. If they're all funny, you'll be funny.

Remember the 80/20 rule? You don't need to be memorizing all sorts of statistics and regimens. Just focus on limiting your fats, carbs, proteins, sodium and sugar. This is an easy template to follow, even if you're a busy professional who is always going to restaurants.

This is what I do. I ask for a chicken breast, not cooked in butter, and a side of steamed broccoli or veggies. Now I have some lean fat and clean protein from the chicken and I've got the complex carbohydrates from the broccoli. This will supply my body all day with energy. It's not about scarcity at all. It's just about eating the right foods. As investors, we look at numbers. As humans, we need to be looking at the food numbers to see what's really going on.

Improve Your Diet, Improve Your Life

I haven't been sick in years. People get sick all around me every winter. Not me. I'm not interested in getting sick. hug sick people all the time, and I don't get sick because I have a powerful immune system. I have an amazing immune system because I've been taking care of it for years. When you do this, your productivity goes way up. You can get more done in less time when you've got a clean mind and a clean body. In addition to increased productivity, other benefits include:

- Better Sleep
- Longevity
- More Energy
- Better Sex
- Faster Healing
- Feeling Better on a Daily Basis

Your insurance rates will also be cheaper. People complain about insurance costs but eat things like processed bologna and white bread. Look at the label for white bread and it says bleached flour as the number one ingredient. Why would you eat bleach? It doesn't make sense.

For me, the biggest benefit of being healthy has been better sex. When you are fat you actually have a smaller penis. According to several health journals, you lose an inch of visible penis for every 30 pounds you are overweight. Your penis is a sponge for blood. If that blood has to go to other places of the body and take care of the fat, this sponge is going to shrink—literally.

The good news is you regain this inch if you lose the 30 pounds. This should be enough motivation to take your health seriously. You're going to have better sex if you're taking care of your body. Everything is tied in to your health. I couldn't write this book and leave this stuff out. But when you see me at the next workshop don't come up to me and say, "Hey, because of you my dick's an inch longer." You can keep that to yourself.

In summary, poison is poison. It doesn't matter how it's wrapped. Look at what's in your food. If it has ingredients you don't know how to pronounce, don't eat it. I am a fan of one-ingredient food. Sweet potatoes, broccoli, fish . . . the fewer the ingredients, the better it is for you. The price of the better food is an investment in a better life and will reduce cost in so many other areas. When you're going through the grocery store, be cautious of anything in a box or a bag. You want it to be natural and clean.

"Let food be thy medicine, and medicine be thy food."
- Hippocrates

Health Savings Account (HAS)

By keeping our bodies healthy, we can now move into some more strategies for making the current healthcare system work for you. The rising cost of healthcare impacts people across the country. The cost of healthcare is going up between 30 and 100 percent a year. It's out of control, and it's causing financial turmoil for a lot of people. Not only is the cost going up, but also the coverage is going down.

Even worse, most people sign up for a Flexible Spending Account (FSA) with their employer. In a Flexible Spending Account, money gets taken out of each paycheck and put into this account to cover healthcare costs. If you don't have any health care costs, then you lose this money.

If you don't use it, you lose it. Who wins in that scenario? The insurance company wins. We want you to win, don't we? We want you to be able to avoid this financial trap, so consider a Health Savings Account (HSA).

In a Health Savings Account, when you put your money in it is there until you spend it. You get a tax deduction for your contribution, and it grows tax-free. If it's invested in real estate, for example, that growth is tax-free. It gets better.

Any distributions for your health care coming out of the HSA are tax-free as well. This. This is what's really exciting. Think about this. Right now, you can contribute $6,750 a year into your Health Savings Account. Now, if you're a healthy person, you don't have a high cost every year for healthcare. This money is going to stay there and grow. I encourage you to start expanding your thought process so you can have your future health care covered.

Say your HSA has $6,750 in it from your first year of contributing. You can now create an LLC to partner with your HSA. This allows you to produce cash flow using your HSA. I recommend real estate. Go buy a property, fix it up, and rent it out for a profit. You can only contribute up to $6,750 a year in earned income to your HSA, but the contributions of cash flow tied to your HSA is uncapped. The cash flow, the profits are not capped. They are unlimited! You can put as much cash flow and profits into your HAS as you can. The only thing capped is earn income contributions.

Here's another idea. Invest in seller financing properties. In this scenario, you buy the property directly from the homeowner and keep their mortgage in place. You make the payments on their behalf instead of paying a mortgage payment to the bank.

Use your initial $6,750 to make a down payment on a seller financing property. When you rent it out, any amount of money above the mortgage payment goes into your HSA as cash flow. Say you go to sell this property and its value has risen $50,000. All those proceeds go back into the HSA. You now have created a nice nest fund to invest in more properties and truly multiply your income.

Now what's the point of an HSA? The point is to take care of your health. The big difference between HSAs and health insurance is the HSA works for you when it comes to taxes on your health. Many services not covered through the insurance companies are a valid health expense. Your HSA will pay for those expenses. Things like vision and dental expenses and emergency occurrences are paid from this account. But there are other things too. Say you want a massage. Go for a massage every week or every other day, according to your schedule. You get to pay for those massages out of your HSA and get a write-off for it.

Depending on your insurance policy, any cost over your deductible, you pay 20 percent and the insurance company pays 80 percent. Once you are out of pocket over $13,000, the insurance company pays for the rest of the healthcare costs. Most plans also have a yearly cap on coverage. If you have health insurance, make sure this cap is at least $1 million.

What makes matters worse is those who have insurance and want to write off health care costs face more restrictions than those with an HSA. With health insurance, you can only write off costs which exceed 10 percent of your adjusted gross income. Trying to itemize deductions for healthcare as a W-2 employee is stacked against you. Say your AGI is $60,000 and you had $6,001 in healthcare costs. You could only write off $1. With an HSA, you can write off every single dollar spent from this account. This is how you take control and take back what's yours.

"Health is not a condition of matter, but of mind."
- Mary Baker Eddy

If you want to know how some people get to write off things like cough drops and toothpaste, it's because they buy these things with an HSA. Your HSA comes with a debit card, so all you have to do is swipe your card and keep track of your purchases.

Anything involved in caring for your health can be bought with an HSA. This includes everyday items such as cough drops, toothpaste, aspirin, mouthwash and toilet paper. You can even write off health seminars if they're related to a condition for which you've been diagnosed. If the seminar is in a different city, you can write off the travel to the seminar as well.

When you start implementing the strategies we've discussed, you can eventually end up with an HSA that contributes to itself without you contributing any earned income. For the first few years your goal is to contribute the $6,750 max to build up your account. You then use this tax-free money to start buying real estate, and the cash flow from these assets fund your HSA for as long as you have them.

Your HSA could end up outliving you if you follow this strategy. This could perpetuate for decades. You can get hundreds of thousands, even millions, into your HSA with this strategy. When it comes time for a major healthcare cost, it is covered through your HSA.

Did you know a lot of healthcare providers would rather take cash than go through the hassle of billing insurance companies? They may even offer a discount to people who pay cash. A payment from an HSA counts as a cash payment, so ask your healthcare provider if they offer a cash discount. In this scenario, you get a discount on your health care and get a tax write off. It's incredible!

Let's look at my buddy Jon as an example. Jon is a hard worker. He is sincere, honest, and has always showed up early and stayed late. He's a great guy. He contributed to his work environment and his community. Jon had a baby, and one day his baby got incredibly sick. Throughout his years on the job, he has been putting money away. He had built up tens of thousands of dollars, but he didn't have the money in an HSA.

When John's son became ill, he had to leave his job. He stopped earning income and his cash pile started to deplete. The costs eventually got so bad that he had to sell everything and move back into his parents' basement.

> *"A healthy attitude is contagious but don't wait*
> *to catch it from others. Be a carrier."*
> *- Tom Stoppard*

Now he has an HSA specifically for his son. Inside his HSA are rental properties to produce cash flow. When a healthcare cost comes up, the assets from his HSA cover the bill. These assets will only grow as his son gets older. It's an incredible setup.

You can even use a traditional insurance plan to grow your HSA. Switch to a plan with a higher deductible and lower monthly premium. Take the difference between your old premium and new premium and contribute it to your HSA each month. It will continue to build up. If you don't use it, the money continues to grow because it's now stored in your HSA. It'll lower your monthly obligation and give you the chance to grow your HSA through investing in real estate and other insurable assets. We want assets to continually produce cash flow and fund your health care. It's an incredible strategy and we've only hit the tip of the iceberg. Get educated on real estate investing before adding rental properties to your HAS. Be responsible.

Take back your existence or die like a punk.

Cheat Code #6
PROTECT THE BASE

"Rule number 1 - Never Lose Money.
Rule number 2 - Don't forget rule number 1"
- Warren Buffet

There are two teams in the game Capture the Flag. Each team has a flag to protect and the objective is to capture the other team's flag. While it's important to reach for the opposing team's flag, defense is what will win the game. There will always be someone coming for your flag. It's your job to protect it.

Your flag translates to your business, your family and your property. Once you've set up your base, you must protect and secure it. The best way to do it is through having the proper insurance. Insurance is all about transferring risk. How much insurance is enough? You don't really know until something happens where you must use the insurance. My training helped me understand you want the most insurance coverage. Insurance exists to transfer risk.

Ask how much risk you want to transfer. Or, how much risk do you want to take yourself. People misunderstand insurance is not about saving money on the monthly premium. You don't want to overpay, but what's more important is what is being covered and how much is being covered.

As a responsible entrepreneur and wealth builder, there are a couple of key insurance policies you should have. The key phrase is, "Pay for the inconsequential and insure the catastrophic." Have this insurance coverage:

- Auto
- Property
- Disability
- Health
- Life
- Business

When insurance companies run their algorithms and risk assessment, they are deciding how much they're going to insure and what it will cost you on a monthly basis. More often than not, they're looking at frequency of claims instead of the amount of the claim. Raising your deductible is paying for the inconsequential. You pay for the damage and the risk up to a certain point. Once the cost of the event goes above the predetermined point, the insurance policy kicks in.

Auto Insurance Example

I've learned I can up my deductible from $250 to $1,000 and actually double my coverage for about the same money. Instead of having $100,000/300,000 for my uninsured/under-insured motorist coverage ($250 deductible), I double my coverage to $250,000/500,000 and pay up to $1,000 of damage in a one-year period. Another bonus from raising the coverage is it qualifies me to get an umbrella policy. Umbrella policies are pretty darn cheap. To get a $5 million umbrella policy, it cost me about $1,000 a year. It covers anything the auto policy wouldn't cover. If the auto policy covers up to $500,000, the umbrella covers $500,000 to $5 million.

What gives you peace of mind? It's main question. Some people claim they never thought about insurance and so they have peace of mind. That's called ignorance is bliss. It's not the kind of peace of mind you want. What you want is an awareness of all the risks and a decision about where you will transfer the risk to give you peace of mind. You don't want to worry about the risks. You want to be aware of it and have a plan so you aren't caught off guard.

Not having the right auto coverage is something that can bite people in the ass the most. One of my lawyer buddies was telling me about his client, a real estate agent. Since part of the agent's job is to drive people around and show them properties, it is part of their business risk. This real estate agent got the cheapest policy. When their client got injured in her car during an accident, she was in trouble. She had the wrong type of insurance. She learned her mistake when she went to use the policy to pay for the hospital. The insurance company wouldn't pay because the agent didn't follow the rules to have business insurance when conducting business in her car. It was devastating to the agent, to their business and to their professional reputation.

As an entrepreneur, if you have clients in your car, double check if you have the right kind of coverage. When you're talking to your insurance agent, tell them what you do, what kind of business you are doing and how many miles you drive. Make sure your agent is aware. If they are casual about it, fire them and get a better agent. You need an agent who is going to go to bat for you. You want someone who will push back when the insurance company is hesitant about paying. Get an agent to represent you and really help you out when you need it. The A-Team agents read between the lines and double-check your coverage. When they make sure everything is in place, you can go out and conduct your business without question of your security. Your business may be selling houses. Their business is getting you the right coverage. Make sure they are doing their job.

Simply driving is one of the riskiest things you do, even if you don't have clients in the car. Yet many people are under-insured with their auto. Other people are driving around without insurance or pulling stunts like hit-and-runs. These people can total your car. You want to have the right coverage to protect yourself from their negligence.

Property Insurance

People have excellent property insurance coverage. Garrett Gunderson was goofing around and said, "Hey man, if you're lacking in auto insurance and get into a car accident, just make sure to drive

them over to your property so your property insurance can kick in."
Obviously it was a joke. But people do cover their property more
than their auto. There is substantially more risk associated with our
auto. Your property doesn't move around the city and encounter
hundreds of humans every day.

With property insurance, it's important you document the
actual property you have inside. If your house burns down, you lose
the sticks and bricks property, but you also lost the personal property.
It's easy to do by just walking around taking pictures or video. Store
the images in the cloud or save a hard copy at a location away from
your home. If anything happens, submit the video and they will not
argue. When you have a video walkthrough, the insurance company
will pay out within a matter of weeks rather than going back and
forth for months and months and still not getting what you are
asking them for because you have no proof of the stuff lost in the
fire. Documentation makes filing a claim much easier and faster for
both parties.

Disability Insurance

What would you do if you had a stroke and could not work?
Until I got some information and quotes about disability insurance, I
had not thought about it. If my brain stopped working to a point
where I can't have a conversation, I wouldn't be able to go to
meetings and run some of my business. I could still enjoy some
aspects of life, but if I couldn't collect on a sale, how am I ever going
to get paid. Disability insurance kicks in and replaces the income. It's
a type of insurance critical to look at. They are willing to take on the

risk of replacing your income if you get hurt and bet against you losing your ability to produce income.

It only works for operational income. If you have tons of passive income with one hundred thousand in rental income, that is your disability insurance. One of your goals as a successful entrepreneur is to build up your passive income, right? Income from your assets, residual and passive income, replaces your active income and will eventually work yourself out of qualifying for disability insurance.

Disability insurance is different than accidental death or dismemberment. One of my friends lost a finger on the job site. They measure the exact piece of finger lost, down to the millimeter and used some equation to pay him for the amount of finger lost. We're not looking for this type of insurance. It is cheap and nit-picky. There are so many ways to accidentally disqualify yourself for it. Know the difference between disability insurance and accidental death and dismemberment insurance.

Life Insurance

I am a big believer in life insurance. I think it's important to get both term and whole life insurance. With term, you can get a large death benefit for a small monthly premium. With whole life insurance, you get a growing cash value over time. It's guaranteed to be used because you are going to die. With auto and property insurance, you may go your entire life and never need to use them. The same is true with disability and health insurance. But with life insurance, you know you will die.

You don't want to leave your loved ones with a burden. Ask yourself if you want your family to have a worse lifestyle, the same or a better lifestyle if you pass on early. Life insurance is one of the most responsible things you can do for your family and generations to come.

When I signed up last year, I felt so amazing about having it. Just knowing if I screwed up for some reason and I die, not only will my wife be taken care of, but my mom will also be taken care of. After all, I got into the automotive industry to help my mom. I was tired of seeing her struggle in life. I have always been interested in helping her. So part of my reason to get life insurance was the ability to provide for her in case something catastrophic happens to me.

Business Insurance

You need to understand the risks of running a business. Some of the stuff you say could be misconstrued and someone might want to sue you for it. If you have a business insurance policy to cover your errors and omissions, you're covered for something catastrophic. At the end of the day, we don't want to think about doom and gloom. That's not the point of insurance. It's about protecting your base.

"At the end of the day the goals are simple. Safety and Security"
- Jodi Rell

You've been working your butt off for years and years, maybe even decades. You've gained things, assets and knowledge. Your human life value is irreplaceable. Going back to life insurance, if you were to pass on, how much money could you have made in the next

10, 20, 30 years if you stayed alive? That's what life is there to replace.

What gives you peace of mind?

I have peace of mind knowing my car and my house are covered to the max. If I get injured or disabled, my income is covered. If I die, people I care about will financially benefit. If I make mistakes in my business, I am covered there too. I sleep like a baby.

Estate Planning

In America right now, less than 50 percent of people have a will or trust. That is insane. It's important to plan for your estate. If you were to pass on early, the court will be forced to settle your affairs. It would mean costs for the courts, attorneys, processing, inheritance and estate taxes. If you don't have your trust, will and estate put together, your successors have to figure out what to do when you die.

What if you get injured to the point you are not able to make your own decisions? Maybe you're on life support? There are directives you can and should put in place for that. You want to make sure all your hard work continues to provide assistance to future generations.

Think about it in these terms: Your business and assets are like a campfire. It provides light, warmth and security. When you die, would you pass out individual logs to each family member? If you did you wouldn't have a fire anymore. You would have a bunch of people holding logs burning their hands.

Unfortunately most estate plans are designed to break up the assets and pass them out to the inheritors. Instead, design a will and trust to maintain the fire. In the future, when family members need what the fire provides, they can take some and still leave the fire intact. The proper arrangement provides a fire for many generations so they can benefit from your hard work and sacrifice. I want to thank Andrew Howell for helping me understand the importance of proper estate planning philosophies. BONUS: Visit MichaelAHuggins.com, register this book and you can watch a quick video training about estate planning.

Quick Recap:

- Get insurance and be happy you're transferring risk
- Insurance companies are there to take on the risk
- Don't just go for the cheapest policy
- Ask your CPA how you can write off as many costs as possible and transfer risk all day
- Ask about your umbrella policies to get the extra coverage

Insurance companies do a really good job of advertising about saving money by switching here and there. But saving money is the second priority. The first priority is to get as much coverage as possible. One reason I like insurance is because they are privately held companies. They are not necessarily government entities. They are in it for the business. They're in it for the profit, just like you. So they aren't going to screw up and run their business into the ground. Take insurance seriously.

Business Choices

Asset protection means taking care of what you've already built and protecting what you will build in the future. If there is a mistake you make accidentally or some partner makes a mistake, you want to make sure no one can take what you've built or your future business.

Consider both Operational Flow and Personal Protection.

Remember the difference between operating as an employee with a W-2 mindset compared to a business owner with a CEO mindset? As a business owner, you need to look at operational stuff like buying and selling goods, holding property, supplying a service.

The Personal Protection side involves personal stuff like your house, your car, your life, your mind and your abilities. You want to create a shield for those things from your business operations and the business liabilities. With a business, you have decided to accept a certain amount of risk. You are no longer a W-2 employee as a human resource to them. You are no longer disposable to the company. Understand your own value. It's why you started a business and get paid what you're worth. You are your greatest asset, not the time you put into the job necessarily.

Entity Structure of the Business

You will want to carefully consider how to set up your business as a sole-proprietor, LLC, S-corp or C-corp. Always consult competent legal counsel in your decision.

It is common mistake to think attorneys are expensive. I

encourage you to switch the thinking and realize not using an attorney could be a hundred tunes more expensive if you make a mistake. Lawyers are $300-400/hr. Without proper guidance, understanding and strategy, you could easily make a $30,000-40,000 mistake. To me, it's the same mindset of thinking oil changes are too expensive. Neglecting the oil changes will cause you to need an engine replaced. Take little steps along the way to take care of what you have.

Sole-Proprietor

By far, the easiest way to set up a business is as a sole proprietor—but it doesn't create *any* protection for you personally. There's no real set up fees. You just claim your name as a company name and go open a separate bank account and you're in business. Running it is pretty easy too. You are your own boss. You buy and sell and make your money. It just goes into the business account. That's it. You pay your bills out of the account and it's pretty easy. You're in full control of managing the business as a sole proprietor.

This set up sounds good when people are starting out. This type of business only shut down if you stop doing business or you die. To some, this sounds terrible. If you die and the business is doing well, why would the business shut down? It's a reason to be cautious about sole proprietorships.

What about taxation? The business entity of a sole proprietorship is not taxed. The owner is taxed. Any money generated in the business shows up on the individual tax return and taxes are paid based on the income. There are no tax benefits so you pay self-employment tax which is currently 15.3 percent. That's a lot. Out of every $100 earned, $15.30 goes out to the government because you are self-employed. Another reason we don't like sole proprietorships.

When you need capital, you as the owner supply it to the sole proprietorship. Venture capitalists don't invest in them. Many banks look at you, the business owner and not the business itself. If they give you a loan, it is to you not the company. It's easy to operate because it is much like you did as a W-2 employee.

Limited Liability Corporation (LLC)

Let's talk about the wonderful world of LLCs. They are a corporation and the name stands for Limited Liability Corporation. To start it up, you must file with the state and there are costs involved in it. You have to file your business name and have a registered agent. Then you pay the licensing fee to register it with your county, state and with the federal government. Those are the first fees. Then you pay another fee to make sure a lawyer sets it up for you. Do not attempt to set up your own LLC. Now, I'm not a lawyer. I'm not a CPA. I'm not a tax attorney. I'm not a financial planner. I just listen to all those guys and gals and I take notes. I pay them for advice and counsel. Now I'm passing it onto you. Usually to pay a lawyer to set an LLC up for you, you're looking at a $300-700 fee.

Members inside the LLC are typically not liable for the debts and disasters occurring in the LLC. You get to keep the business separate from your personal life. The administrative requirements are pretty low. They don't make you do quarterly payroll or anything like that. Because of the way it is set up, the administration duties are similar to your day-to-day operations. An LLC is pretty easy admin stuff.

When you set up the LLC, you get together with any members and managers to decide who owns what as a percentage of what, who's the manager and who's a member. Also decide if it is a managed by the manager or the members manage the LLC.

There are two extra forms you get with your LLC. First, you will have Articles of Incorporation which spells out the company name, the entity's identification number and the address where the business is registered. If someone wants to contact you as the business, they can send you mail at the address. The other form is called the Operating Agreement (the OA). The OA tells you everything else such as who does what, who's in charge of what, when and where, what happens if …

My CPA and tax attorney set up the OA with other partners, I should "Negotiate like enemies so you can operate like friends." What it means is get clear of every "what if" before going into business so when those things happen, you just refer back to the OA. There's no dispute because ultimately the emotion has been taken out of the decision-making process.

Some of the questions you need to answer are:
- What if a member dies?
- What if a member wants to get out?
- What if they want to sell or have a buy-out?
- What if there's a car crash with the company car?
- What if there are overdrafts?

- What if we become insolvent?
- What if we want to bring in another partner?
- What if the company needs to make purchases?
- What if we need a mediator?
- What if we're partnering on a property and the value goes down and we can't refinance?
- What if there's a disagreement between two members?
- Who helps to settle or mediate?

Figure out all those what ifs ahead of time. Put it on paper and then you can operate as friends. You know all the what ifs are covered. You don't lay in bed wondering what your partner would do if this happens. Instead of thinking about that kind of stuff, you can be productive with your thoughts. Get it all down on paper in the Operating Agreement so you can refer back to it when needed. A key point to remember is peace of mind is the biggest aid in a productive mindset.

The OA also spells out how to transfer ownership. To capitalize your LLC, you can sell off interests. If the LLC is going to buy some property, you could say, "You can have 10 percent of the property for X number of dollars." When you get 10 percent of the property, you get 10 percent of the cash flow, 10 percent of the tax pass-through stuff, 10 percent of the growth etc. It's how you capitalize. You sell shares and then exchange the ownership for cash and put the cash in the company's bank account.

Be aware having more than ten members may violate some securities laws. You can have too many people in the LLC. As you continue to sell shares, just make sure you communicate with the lawyer each and every time.

LLCs are pretty easy to operate. There's an extra benefit in about 10 states where you can have multiple LLCs under one umbrella LLC. In those states you can have 10 LLCs under one umbrella LLC and file one tax return. In other states, you have to do a return for each LLC.

Drawing a comparison to the sole proprietorship, which shuts down when you die, LLCs go on in perpetuity. They last as long as you continue to fill out the state registration every year. A few states do have exceptions to the rule, but not many. You may wonder if there are any tax benefits in an LLC. There are not. You still have to pay the 15.3 percent self-employment tax, plus other taxes related to the LLC. Each member of the LLC gets a K-1 tax form saying how much money the LLC made for the member. The number gets added to your own personal tax return. Again, there are not tax benefits from an LLC.

Another good idea is to name your law firm as the registered agent of you LLC when you create it. Then, if people want to sue you, they see a lawyer is your registered agent. Other lawyers will know it will be harder to get a settlement and may not want to do the lawsuit anymore. Little things like this make a big difference. Ask your lawyer if they'll be a registered agent for you.

The LLC is an incredible way to protect your assets. You have the opportunity to grow and expand these businesses to your heart's desire. As long as you follow some simple rules, you will have asset protection and you will also have the privacy you want. LLCs can own other LLCs, so you can start to stack those and maintain the privacy.

Privacy is a big deal, especially when you get into holding rental properties. You don't really want your renters to know who you are or where you live. You just want them to pay the rent on time. Your agreement is: you maintain a safe, clean affordable housing. Their agreement is: they pay for it on time. They don't need to know who you are or where you live. Do the proper structuring and your corporate maintenance to protect your privacy.

S Corporation

The S corp is similar to the LLC in many ways. You pick a name and file it with the state. You have some fees to pay and it's more expensive to set up. Instead of the $300-700 you pay a lawyer for the LLC, you can easily spend $1,500-3,000 to set up the S corp.

Beware of "out-of-state corporation." Only set up entities in states where you live and do business. There are other technical details you want to make sure are set up correctly. Again, please use competent legal advice. In the S corp, instead of having members and managers, you have shareholders. Shareholders elect a board of directors. They pick the CEO. CFO, COO, CMO and eh CLO. It's important your board of directors doesn't have an even number of people. If you have four people and the vote is split two to two, no decision is made. Have three, five or seven so the majority can always come to a decision and move forward.

One of the nice benefits many take is making family members in the corporate positions. Instead of the conversations you used to have as an employee about how crappy the job was or how dumb the boss is, your family is involved in the operation of the company. When family members are the treasurer and secretary and the board of directors, you start talking about prosperity, making money and passing on your experience and your legacy.

You are required to have annual meetings and have records of the annual minutes. These meetings can be anywhere in the world. Instead of having a vacation, you have a business meeting with your board of directors and officers. It's clearly a business expense to travel anywhere in the world. You sure couldn't justify a trip as a W-2 employee to the IRS. As an S corp, get this huge benefit.

In managing the S corp, shareholders elect the directors who manage the business activities in a voting process. The S corp does not expire when you die. S corps are not subject to a corporate tax. No double taxation. No corporate tax.

What about self-employment tax? In the S corp, you pay self-employment tax on the salary portion of what is distributed to you. The other members are responsible for their share. My tax attorney told me to do a salary-dividend split. While the salary is subject to self-employment tax, the dividend is not. I split it with one third of the distribution as salary and two-thirds as a dividend. That way, I eliminate self-employment tax on two-thirds of what I receive. How cool is that?

Continuing to take a dividend can be a red flag to the IRS. It's not always a good idea. Depending on what kind of business you're in and also if you want to get more houses, more cars or contribute to retirement accounts. All those monies have to be salary money.

You can't put money in an IRA with dividend money.

Remember if you want to buy a car with a loan, the lender will give you the loan based on your salary, not the total of the money you receive from the S corp. You may think it's a good idea to save on taxes by showing little or no salary, but the lender will say you don't make enough money to get the loan. The highest paid, smartest attorneys I hang out with recommend one-third salary and two-thirds dividend as the most effective strategy.

You can transfer ownership, but the IRS requires a specific way to do it. It's more technical than the OA used in the LLC where you can simply add someone on. Recently, I had a partner in an LLC and we weren't interested in working together anymore. We just got one piece of paper saying, in effect, transfer this guy's ownership rights over to Michael. We signed and notarized it, recorded it with the state, and now I am 100 percent owner. That was it. I didn't have to go through any IRS stuff to do it. With S corporations, it's a little more technical.

When you want to raise capital for an S corp, you create stock and shares of stock. Only people can buy shares of your S corp. Other corporations can't buy shares of your corporation. Sometimes this rule can be unattractive. If you're trying to work with other companies and they like to buy shares of your stuff, the S corp is going to be limited to only sole proprietors—or people with a social security number.

As far as ease of operation, the S corp has a few extra steps. We mentioned the board of directors, officers and annual meetings earlier. Also, the IRS wants to see quarterly payroll tax reporting. The

S corp is a little more expensive to operate. But in the end, if you're saving a lot on self-employment tax, the savings could be way more than the cost of doing the quarterly stuff, annual maintenance and corporate maintenance.

C Corporation

In most ways, the C corp is the same as the S corp when it comes to forming it and filing with the state. It is a little more expensive though. It gives you a good protection for personal liability to protect your personal stuff from your company stuff. Administrative requirements are pretty much the same. You elect the board of directors and officers. Then the directors manage the business activities. When you die, the corporation continues on, which is incredibly important when you're in multiple states and continuing to grow. You don't want the business to be shut down just because you die.

When it comes to taxation, there is a required corporate tax for C corporations. Also, dividends are taxed as regular income to the shareholders. There is double taxation. The business is taxed at the corporate level and then again on the distribution to the shareholders when you issue dividends. The double taxation is an issue for a lot of people. Salary, just like in an S corp, is subject to self-employment tax in a C corp.

The C corp is ideal for big business because transferring ownership and selling shares/stocks is incredibly easy with this structure. Venture capitalists are more interested in funding companies set up as C corporations because the shares can be easily transferred. Remember raising capital and selling stocks/shares is subject to securities laws. Understanding the SEC laws is incredibly important. Use a lawyer. If you make a mistake, you can get into a lot of trouble and get fined. They could shut you down. Just follow the rules and talk to a competent CPA. Okey-dokey?

As far as operation, you're going to pay a CPA and a tax attorney to make sure all the regular filings, payroll taxes and distribution tax is all in check. Those guys and gals aren't necessarily cheap, but they sure are worth it. Definitely worth it.

Day-to-day operations of a corporation are totally different than with a sole proprietorship. Almost every successful millionaire networks. They are looking to network with other business owners and CEOs. When you graduate from the sole proprietor you become a CEO and it changes the way you look at yourself. It changes the way you show up in the world. You take more responsibility for your business.

It's your responsibility to get educated on this stuff. It's up to you because ultimately you're going to be the one funding your retirement accounts, your college funds, all the business accounts, your trust and your life insurance.

The Importance of the Corporate Veil

As you know, there is a lot more information out there about how to operate as an employee, but not much training about how to operate a business. Something you must understand is there is a thing called the corporate veil. It is a shield between your business activities and your personal activities. To maintain the corporate veil, you must keep the stuff separate.

People will "pierce" the corporate veil, sometimes by accident, by neglecting some key rules of engagement. Let's cover some of those activities so you know what not to do.

Rule number one: Don't blend your accounts.

Rule number two: Don't blend your accounts.

If you have a business account and you buy personal stuff like groceries, you have blended the two. Vice versa, if you start buying stuff for the business with your personal account. If you need to buy something personal, you just transfer money from your business account into your personal account—then you buy the stuff. If you don't transfer the money, it's called "unity of interest." The courts will look at the activity and say you aren't operating as a business because you are blending the two accounts.

It's a big deal because if you blend your accounts, you can lose your asset protection. Another term they use is co-mingling funds. You don't want to co-mingle funds. Avoid it at all costs.

Documenting is also important when you put money from your personal income into starting up the company. If you don't document putting the personal income into your business, it's considered the same as using your business income to pay for personal stuff. Just document the movement of money and you should be good to go. No co-mingling.

Pay attention to how you sign documents or it can become another way to hurt the corporate veil. I learned this mistake from experience. I did a real estate transaction using a private money lender. I took on a six-figure debt in order to purchase the property and rehab it, with plans to sell at a profit. The project and timeline didn't go as planned. We weren't able to sell it the way we originally thought. When we went back to review who was responsible for what, I found my big mistake.

I had signed the trustee note in my own name, instead of my name as manager of the LLC. Because I didn't put the qualifier of manager of the LLC, it created a "personal guarantee." It meant I would be personally liable if he didn't get paid back. He could foreclose and sell the property at an auction. He could sue me personally for any difference between what was owed and the auction price. It all happened because I didn't sign the document with my role in the LLC. Always, always, always sign as the LLC. It's such a big deal.

One of the big reasons why you have an entity and the asset protection structure of the LLC, is to keep personal separate from business. At all costs, avoid doing personal guarantees. Sometimes a lender will want a personal guarantee. You've got to negotiate like crazy to avoid the personal guarantee in case the business fails. Protecting your family from your business stuff and also protecting your business from your family stuff.

The corporate veil dissolves if you do fraudulent, illegal things or lie about where money is coming from or where it is going. If you do anything like that, it will remove the corporate veil and allow debtors to access your personal stuff.

If you take money out of the company in any way besides what is outlined in the operating agreement, it will also dissolve the corporate veil. If you stick to the operating agreement, you've got a shield 100 percent. As soon as you start taking money out in a different way, the shield starts to get weak and people can start to access your personal assets.

You cannot accept a distribution that makes the company insolvent. When you just take money and bankrupt the company, the corporate veil is pierced and they'll come after your personal assets. Some people have tried to push assets out of the LLC and then declare bankruptcy on the LLC. But when it's done, all the wiring of funds, all the activity is tracked. The paper trail will show you did it on purpose and then, no more corporate veil. You are personally liable for all of the debt.

Loss of the corporate veil happens whether it was your idea or not. If you accept a distribution of cash or assets when it results in the LLC becoming insolvent, the acceptance could pierce the corporate veil and your personal assets are at risk. Sometimes people do it by accident. You've got to pay attention.

At the end of the day, you just make sure you have a bulletproof case to show you kept your business and personal stuff separate. That's it. When faced with a challenge as how a judge would look at it. Are you keeping the money separate or is it co-mingled? If you get caught up in a lawsuit or get taken to court for some reason, you will have to plead your case.

Real estate is risky. Everything is risky, especially when you're starting out and don't understand it. The risk may not actually be in the investment. When an experienced builder, contractor or real estate agent makes the investment, they understand the functions in the areas where they invest. It's not nearly as risky for them to take on a house as someone who has never ever even looked at real estate or opened up an escrow. The risk is not necessarily in the investment. You get educated and only invest in what you know.

"You have to know what you stand for, not just what you stand against."
- Laurie Halse Anderson

In the end, as long as you follow the rules and maintain separate accounting, you will maintain the corporate veil.

Take back your existence. Or die like a punk.

CHEAT CODE #7
LIFETIME LEARNING

"A love affair with knowledge will never end in heartbreak."
- Michael Garrett Marino

I attribute all of my success to the lessons taught to me during the last six years. I have devoted myself to taking in new information continuously and learning to be a better human. Becoming a lifetime learner is critical to your success. We must create a lifestyle of learning for a lifetime.

Recently I came across a little story to illustrate the importance of lifetime learning. A survey was taken to ask billionaires this question: "If you could have any superpower, what superpower would you pick?" Without knowing how the other answered, both Bill Gates and Warren Buffett said, "The ability to read faster." They wouldn't ask for flight, invisibility, super strength or any other things. They wanted to be able to read faster. They have billions and still want to learn and read more. Learning is part of their lifestyle.

Lifetime learning is what will keep your growth mindset going. When you're in a growth mindset, you ask different questions and you focus on very different things. With a fixed mindset, without lifetime learning, you just go day-to-day and it's all the same.

NOTE: The Merriam-Webster definition of intelligence is, "(1)the ability to learn or understand or deal with new or trying situations; (2) the ability to apply knowledge to manipulate one's environment; (3) the power of knowing as distinguished from the power to feel and to will." Intelligence is a faculty of the mind. It is like muscles of the body. We have to continue to work them out to get stronger and stronger. Imagination is a faculty. Decision is a faculty. Intellect is a faculty. As you continue to work on this stuff, it revolutionizes your life.

Keep evolving and learning because what you don't know will hurt you. You may have heard what you don't know won't hurt you, but this is WRONG. You've got to continue to study and learn. I remember my first mentor, Jody Hill. She said, "Okay—you're ready to be on board with the team and the training. You want to change your life and you want to make a bunch of money. Read these two books and call me as soon as you're done."

I immediately went from goofing around wasting time—to spending every spare minute reading these books. I wanted to be engaged with the millionaires and the investors so I could be plugged in. Continued learning gave me a positive association. I was given this phrase, "The more you know, the more you grow." If you don't grow you're never going to be able to have the lifestyle, relationships, health, fitness, finance, all that crap. You're not going to be able to have it unless you continue to grow. All these little catch phrases started really building up in my mind:

- The more you know, the more you grow.
- The more you learn, the more you earn.
- Leaders are readers.

I was relieved to learn there are no new problems in this world. Any problem you're experiencing in your life, someone solved it and wrote a book about it. You can either spend four, five, ten years trying to solve it yourself, or you could spend four, five, ten hours and learn from someone who spent all those years to figure it out and learn from them. It's great news to know if you are experiencing any sort of problems: depression, communication, violent outbreaks, sadness, getting your feelings hurt, not making money, not getting a girlfriend, you're fat, you can't sleep—all of this stuff is solved by reading.

This lifetime of learning is going to shape you into a better person so you can attract more things and have a bigger mental capacity to solve more problems. Scott Rowe helped me understand the difference by using the four currencies. We have time, we have knowledge, we have relationships and we have money. According to your mindset, you look at these currencies in very different ways. The wealthy look at time as a tool and a reason. The poor look at time as a tool.

Money and Time

This is something I had heard before, but seeing it in a practical format drove the point home. Here's the story when I really learned this lesson. I was at an amusement park on a bright, beautiful, sunny day with some out of town buddies. I wanted to show them a good time. At the first ride, the lines were incredibly long. So I went to the front of the line and learned people had been waiting two hours to go on this ride. Two hours! No way! That meant in 8 hours, we would go on 4 rides and it wouldn't be much fun. I looked for a better way.

The 4 Currencies

	Poor Mindset	Wealthy Mindset
Time	Tool	Reason
Money	Reason	Tool
Knowledge	Limited	Journey
Relationships	Competitive	Cooperative

The doorstep to the temple of wisdom is a knowledge of our own ignorance."
- Benjamin Franklin

I found out about a Fast Pass I could purchase. What I did was used my money as a tool to save time, which was my reason. I wanted to spend time with my colleagues and I was willing to sue my money to get the time. It was interesting because the Fast Pass was 50 bucks and it saved each of us hours. We went straight to the front of the line and rode 12 rides in 4 hours instead of 4 rides in 8 hours. We skipped 1-2 hours 12 times. Okay, if it was only an hour, at 50 bucks it cost us 4 dollars an hour. 4 dollars an hour!

"A healthy attitude is contagious but don't wait to catch it from others.
Be a carrier."
- Tom Stoppard

I started thinking, "Why on earth won't these people in this line we were skipping be willing to wait so long? Why didn't they get a Fast Pass?" It's because of the mentality of time as their tool and thought, "I will spend my time to save money." This experience made me realize I had made a mental switch where I am more comfortable spending money than time. Jim Rohn says, "Days are expensive. If you spend one day, you have one less to spend. I didn't want to spend my time standing in line, so I exchanged the currency of money to get the time.

Example in Parenting

When parents take their kid to daycare and drop them off in the kiddie kennel, their justification is, "I need to go exchange my time for money." This tells the kid they are important, but money is more important. Of course, it's not said in words, but sending them to the playpen to hang out with other kids in the little kid cage while the parent goes to another place to get some money.

People are doing their best, but ignorance is not bliss. If they knew they could make money from home, or if they knew they could develop a business involving their kid, they'd be doing it. They could make money and have time with the kid. Unfortunately, they didn't pursue the knowledge, they didn't pursue something different, and so they're exchanging their time for money and putting money as more important. Money is their reason.

If you're going to make the switch from poor to wealthy, I strongly encourage you to start to look at money as a tool, not a reason.

"Live as if you were to die tomorrow. Learn as if you were to live forever."
- Mahatma Gandhi

Knowledge - a Journey or a Burden

To the wealthy, knowledge is a journey and have lifetime learning. Wealthy people understand it's a continuous thing. There's more to learn. There's more to expand upon. There are more places on the planet to visit. There are more languages to learn. There's more art to take in. There are more things to learn about your body and relationships and connectivity and God and spirit and universe and vibrations and molecules, food, animals and water. There's so much to learn.

Wealthy people understand it's a journey and it's never going to end. That's why Bill and Warren want to be able to read faster.

Poor people look at knowledge as a burden. They say, "Just give me the diploma and I want to stop learning. Please, let me just get on with it."

Relationships

The wealthy look at relationships as cooperative, whereas poor people look at relationships as competitive. Poor people think there is only one pie. If more people are involved, it cuts into the pie an there's less for everyone. The reason they stay poor is the scarcity mentality. There's no way around it.

Wealthy people understand relationships are cooperative. When we bring more people on, more can get done and we accelerate it. If more can get done and we can accelerate, then everyone gets to share in the profits, benefits, joy and abundance. An abundance mentality makes it so you can share, which means more people are willing to share with you, which means you can get more.

"There is no end to education. It is not that you read a book, pass an examination, and finish with education. The whole of life, from the moment you are born to the moment you die, is a process of learning."
- Jidda Krishnamurti

There are communities of real estate investors all across the country. I encourage you to go investigate with a cooperative mindset. Understand knowledge is a journey and you're there to invest some money and get back your time. Study this. Learn it. Apply the changes needed. If you've gone through a self-inventory and you thought, *Whoo, I need to make some major changes here.* I encourage you to do it. Because if you don't you're going to maintain a victim mentality and you're going to stay poor.

"Things turn out best for the people who make the best of the way things turn out."
- John Wooden

Take back your existence or die like a punk.

Peace out.

DISCLAIMERS

General Disclaimer

The information, services, products, claims, seminar topics, and materials on our Sites are provided "as is" and without warranties of any kind, either expressed or implied. We disclaim all warranties, expressed or implied, including but not limited to implied effectiveness of the ideas or success strategies listed on this site as well as those that are provided in our products or to our participants at our events. The only exception is the guarantees of satisfaction and graduation that are clearly labeled guarantees within our Sites.

Neither we nor any of our respective licensors or suppliers warrant that any functions contained in the Sites will be uninterrupted or error-free, that defects will be corrected, or that the Sites or the server that makes them available are free of viruses or other harmful components. Neither we nor any of our respective licensors or suppliers warrant or make any representations regarding the use or the results of the use of the services, products, information or materials in this site in terms of their correctness, accuracy, reliability, or otherwise.

You (and not we or any of our respective licensors or suppliers) assume the entire cost of all necessary servicing, repair or correction to your system. Applicable law may not allow the exclusion of implied warranties, so the above exclusion may not apply to you.

We do not endorse, warrant or guarantee any speakers, products or services offered on the Sites or those we link to. We are not a party to, and do not monitor, any transaction between users and third party providers of products or services.

Earnings Disclaimer

When addressing financial matters in any of our Sites, videos, newsletters or other content, we've taken every effort to ensure we accurately represent our programs and their ability to improve your life or grow your business. However, there is no guarantee that you will get any results or earn any money using any of our ideas, tools, strategies or recommendations, and we do not purport any "get rich schemes" on any of our Sites. Nothing on our Sites is a promise or guarantee of earnings.

Your level of success in attaining similar results is dependent upon a number of factors including your skill, knowledge, ability, dedication, business savvy, network, and financial situation, to name a few. Because these factors differ according to individuals, we cannot and do not guarantee your success, income level, or ability to earn revenue. You alone are responsible for your actions and results in life and business. Any forward-looking statements outlined on our Sites are simply our opinion and are not guarantees or promises for actual performance.

It should be clear to you that we legally make no guarantees that you will achieve any results from our ideas or models presented on our Sites, and we offer no professional legal, medical, psychological or financial advice.

Indemnification

You agree to indemnify, defend and hold harmless our officers, directors, employees, agents and third parties, for any losses, costs, liabilities and expenses (including reasonable attorneys' fees) relating to or arising out of your use of or inability to use the Site or services, any user postings made by you, your violation of any terms of this Agreement or your violation of any rights of a third party, or your violation of any applicable laws, rules or regulations. We reserve the right, at its own cost, to assume the exclusive defense and control of any matter otherwise subject to indemnification by you, in which event you will fully cooperate with us in asserting any available defenses.

Limitation of Liability

The information, software, products, and services included in or available through the site may include inaccuracies or typographical errors. Changes are periodically added to the information herein. We and/or our suppliers may make improvements and/or changes in the site at any time.

We and/or our suppliers make no representations about the suitability, reliability, availability, timeliness, and accuracy of the information, software, products, services and related graphics contained on the site for any purpose. To the maximum extent permitted by applicable law, all such information, software, products, services and related graphics are provided "as is" without warranty or condition of any kind. We and/or our suppliers hereby disclaim all warranties and conditions with regard to this information, software, products, services and related graphics, including all implied warranties or conditions of merchantability, fitness for a particular purpose, title and non-infringement.

To the maximum extent permitted by applicable law, in no event shall we and/or our suppliers be liable for any direct, indirect, punitive, incidental, special, consequential damages or any damages whatsoever including, without limitation, damages for loss of use, data or profits, arising out of or in any way connected with the use or performance of the site, with the delay or inability to use the site or related services, the provision of or failure to provide services, or for any information, software, products, services and related graphics obtained through the site, or otherwise arising out of the use of the site, whether based on contract, tort, negligence, strict liability or otherwise, even if we or any of our suppliers have been advised of the possibility of damages.

Because some states/jurisdictions do not allow the exclusion or limitation of liability for consequential or incidental damages, the above limitation may not apply to you. If you are dissatisfied with any portion of the site, or with any of these terms of use, your sole and exclusive remedy is to discontinue using the site. Under no circumstances will we be held responsible or liable, directly or indirectly, for any loss or damage that is caused or alleged to have been caused to you in connection with your use of any advice, goods or services you receive from a guest speaker on our Sites or at one of our events. We are also not responsible or liable for any loss or damage that is caused or alleged to have been caused to our guest speakers or content partners in connection with the display of their photo, name, or biography posted on our Sites or in our marketing materials.

No Professional Advice

The information contained in or made available through the Sites (including but not limited to information contained on message boards, in text files, or in chats) cannot replace or substitute for the services of trained professionals in any field, including, but not limited to, financial, medical, psychological, or legal matters. In particular, you should regularly consult a doctor in all matters relating to physical or mental health, particularly concerning any symptoms that may require diagnosis or medical attention. We and our licensors or suppliers make no representations or warranties concerning any treatment, action, or application of medication or preparation by any person following the information offered or provided within or through the Sites.

Neither we nor our partners, or any of their affiliates, will be liable for any direct, indirect, consequential, special, exemplary or other damages that may result, including but not limited to economic loss, injury, illness or death. You alone are responsible and accountable for your decisions, actions and results in life, and by your use of the Sites, you agree not to attempt to hold us liable for any such decisions, actions or results, at any time, under any circumstance.

Links to Third Party Sites/Services

The Site may contain links to other websites ("Linked Sites"). The Linked Sites are not under our control and we are not responsible for the contents of any Linked Site, including without limitation any link contained in a Linked Site, or any changes or updates to a Linked Site. We are providing these links to you only as a convenience, and the inclusion of any link does not imply endorsement by us of the Site or any association with its operators. Certain services made available via the Site are delivered by third party sites and organizations.

By using any product, service or functionality originating from the Site domain, you hereby acknowledge and consent that we may share such information and data with any third party with whom we have a contractual relationship to provide the requested product, service or functionality on behalf of the Site users and customers. We may receive financial or other compensation from your use of some Linked Services.

No Unlawful or Prohibited Use/Intellectual Property

You are granted a non-exclusive, non-transferable, revocable license to access and use the Site strictly in accordance with these terms of use. As a condition of your use of the Site, you warrant to us that you will not use the Site for any purpose that is unlawful or prohibited by these Terms. You may not use the Site in any manner which could damage, disable, overburden, or impair the Site or interfere with any other party's use and enjoyment of the Site. You may not obtain or attempt to obtain any materials or information through any means not intentionally made available or provided for through the Site.

All content included as part of the Service, such as text, graphics, logos, images, as well as the compilation thereof, and any software used on the Site, is our property or our suppliers and protected by copyright and other laws that protect intellectual property and proprietary rights. You agree to observe and abide by all copyright and other proprietary notices, legends or other restrictions contained in any such content and will not make any changes thereto. You will not modify, publish, transmit, reverse engineer, participate in the transfer or sale, create derivative works, or in any way exploit any of the content, in whole or in part, found on the Site.

Our content is not for resale. Your use of the Site does not entitle you to make any unauthorized use of any protected content, and in particular you will not delete or alter any proprietary rights or attribution notices in any content. You will use protected content solely for your personal use, and will make no other use of the content without the express written permission from us and the copyright owner. You agree that you do not acquire any ownership rights in any protected content. We do not grant you any licenses, express or implied, to our intellectual property or our licensors except as expressly authorized by these Terms.

International Users

The Service is controlled, operated and administered by us from our offices within the USA. If you access the Service from a location outside the USA, you are responsible for compliance with all local laws. You agree that you will not use our Content accessed through the Site in any country or in any manner prohibited by any applicable laws, restrictions or regulations.

REGISTER THIS BOOK

Register your book and get free updates and free videos.

Visit www.MichaelAHuggins.com or text your name and email address to 801-899-6001.

When your book is registered you will get updates to this book plus access to videos showing you how to grow your business with strategies from this book. You will also get an invitation to an interactive online webinar to meet the author and his team.

ABOUT THE AUTHOR

Michael A. Huggins has helped numerous people rapidly pay off their debt, create more control over their investments and substantially increase returns on their retirement accounts. He is in high demand as a financial trainer and is known nationwide. As an international speaker, he focuses on helping entrepreneurs become their best selves. With his extensive knowledge in personal development, Michael has coached many into living the life they deserve. As one of the youngest leaders in his community, he has set the bar high for those following, and he will continue to push himself to be the best he can be.

Michael has been trained by well known professionals like Mark Kohler, Garrett Gunderson, John C. Maxwell, Bob Snyder, and Woody Woodward. He's been featured on The Dr. G & Kevin Show and various entrepreneurial blogs.

As a top income earner in the sales and marketing division of a world class educational company, Michael has received several awards for his efforts including 2016 Utah Regional Excelling Leadership Award, 2016 Colorado Regional Leadership Award, and the 2016 Summer in Denver Driving Force Award.

Michael was frustrated and fed up with the tough labor and low pay of his auto-mechanic profession. He felt like he was going nowhere fast. Michael made a conscious decision in his life to master real estate and finance. As a result, his income multiplied 10 fold in just a few short years.

With many years of experience behind him, Michael has mastered the skills of running a successful marketing business. He now runs a team of 220+ people and has had substantial growth over the last 2 years. This heightened income has allowed Michael to follow his dreams. He now has the time and freedom to tinker with race cars, travel the world, and be with his family.

Follow Michael at:

Website: www.MichaelAHuggins.com

Facebook: facebook.com/AuthorMichaelHuggins

Twitter:twitter.com/MHuggins_LLC

Made in the USA
Columbia, SC
08 June 2019